TORPEDO RUN

TORPEDO RUN

TORPEDO RUN

The Story of World War II
Submarine Hero Eugene B. Fluckey

BY DON KEITH

CALIBER

CALIBER

An imprint of Penguin Random House LLC
penguinrandomhouse.com

Copyright © 2022 by Don Keith
Penguin supports copyright. Copyright fuels creativity, encourages diverse
voices, promotes free speech, and creates a vibrant culture. Thank you for
buying an authorized edition of this book and for complying with copyright
laws by not reproducing, scanning, or distributing any part of it in any form
without permission. You are supporting writers and allowing Penguin to
continue to publish books for every reader.

DUTTON and the D colophon are registered trademarks of
Penguin Random House LLC.

LIBRARY OF CONGRESS CATALOGING-IN-PUBLICATION DATA
has been applied for.

ISBN 9780593185971 (paperback)
ISBN 9780593185988 (ebook)

Printed in the United States of America
1st Printing

All photos courtesy of the Naval History and Heritage Command.

While the author has made every effort to provide accurate telephone
numbers, internet addresses, and other contact information at the time of
publication, neither the publisher nor the author assumes any responsibility
for errors or for changes that occur after publication. Further, the publisher
does not have any control over and does not assume any responsibility for
author or third-party websites or their content.

Dedicated to the memory of the 375 officers and 3,131 sailors who lost their lives while serving aboard the fifty-two US Navy submarines lost during World War II.

★ CONTENTS ★

PROLOGUE

The skipper of the submarine USS *Barb* (SS-220) had no intention of accepting his Medal of Honor. Commander Eugene B. Fluckey was honored that he had been recommended for his country's highest award for bravery. Yes, he was proud that the request had been approved by men who knew how difficult the job was. Proud because it would bring tribute and attention to his crew and their considerable accomplishments. But there was a long list of reasons—a thick file of them that Fluckey kept in his briefcase to show to anyone who mattered—why he would not mind being the first recipient in the history of the medal to refuse to accept it.

First, Fluckey firmly believed that such a solemn recognition should be reserved only for those who died in defense of their country. Though things had gotten very tense at times during

Barb's eleventh World War II patrol, Fluckey was still breathing. And the captain's personal favorite bragging point was still valid. Despite the furious action she had faced in his first four patrols as the submarine's skipper, not a single crewmember had suffered a serious injury. Not one man had earned a different medal, a Purple Heart, for having been wounded in combat.

No, Fluckey told his superiors, he would prefer receiving a fourth Navy Cross instead. There was a practical reason for that substitution. By tradition, that would allow him the privilege of nominating thirteen members of his crew for their own awards, including the Silver Star, the Bronze Star, and Letters of Commendation with Ribbons. So far, thanks to his previous three personal Navy Crosses while commanding *Barb*, he had seen that forty-three of his men received recognition for what they had done out there against a fanatical enemy. Those honors had been earned in submarines, the area of the military that already had the highest casualty rate of any in the war. The Medal of Honor, on the other hand, carried only the option for Fluckey to submit for acknowledgment a half dozen of his crew.

There were scheduling conflicts involved, too. President Roosevelt, who had already had several personal encounters with Fluckey and was an unabashed fan of the skipper, wanted to personally award the medal to him, and do it in a White House ceremony before a large contingent of press. It would be good for morale, both military and civilian. However, as it happened, the chief executive was too ill to do so during the time that *Barb's* skipper, with his sub at Mare Island, California, for refit, would be available. The plan was to delay the ceremony until mid-April 1945, which would take Fluckey away from the boat at a crucial time, while in the final stages of preparing for her next patrol. It would also require calling in his executive officer early from stateside leave, something Fluckey was reluctant to do.

There was another long-standing tradition associated with the honor that the skipper was determined to avoid. Anytime a living recipient was awarded the Medal of Honor, it was typical that he was not sent right back to combat duty. There were public relations opportunities to exploit. Morale visits to be made. War bond drives to support. And not being put back into harm's way so quickly was seen as a reward for such gallant service.

Fluckey would not hear of that! He had big plans for his fifth patrol on *Barb*. By hook and crook, he had convinced the Navy to allow him to carry a rocket launcher and a supply of rockets. He intended to test his theories about the use of such a weapon from the deck of a submarine. He wanted to demonstrate how he could capitalize on the stealth of the sub, a vessel that could creep up to point-blank range, launch an attack on shore-based targets, then flee and dive. No other warship could do that. He had the perfect objective in mind already, too.

In addition, Fluckey had formulated another unusual method for an assault on a most unorthodox but enticing target. That radical idea he had not yet shared with anyone else, though. Not even his executive officer or crew.

As it happened, Eugene Fluckey was unable to trade his Medal of Honor for a fourth Navy Cross. He did manage, however, to negotiate his way back to the war, but only after going way up the chain of submarine command to do so. Admiral Charles Lockwood, commander of Submarine Force, US Pacific Fleet, had tentatively promised the skipper a fifth patrol. By this time in the war, sub skippers were being limited to only four runs without a break because of the stress of such duty. But Fluckey would be approved to make his fifth trip only if things went well with *Barb*'s fourth patrol.

Things had gone very well on that run. Medal of Honor–worthy. Lockwood sent Fluckey a personal message as the submarine was headed home. It said, in part: "The all-time all-timer! Aggressive, tenacious, daring, unique, extremely injurious to the enemy. PS. Congratulations from all of us and the whole U.S.A."

Clearly, Admiral Lockwood could not go back on his promise now. Not even if his star skipper was to receive the Medal of Honor and automatic entitlement to a "safe" patrol.

The *Barb*, under Fluckey's command, had just completed one of the most successful submarine war patrols of World War II. Now, with her captain still fuming about the Navy's insistence on awarding him the medal, the sub was on her way to mayhem again.

And *Barb* was plying westward through the Pacific with Eugene Fluckey at the helm, one of only eight submariners to be awarded the Medal of Honor.

This fifth run—the one that almost did not happen—would prove to be another rousing success for Fluckey and *Barb*. It would also include some of the most unique battle action, not only in the history of the "Silent Service," but in the whole of naval warfare.

It was battle action initiated by a man whose life was turned around when, as a freckle-faced boy listening to his cat-whisker crystal radio set, he heard and heeded some strong advice from a man nicknamed Silent Cal.

TORPEDO RUN

CHAPTER ONE

"NOTHING CAN TAKE THE PLACE OF PERSISTENCE"

Eugene Bennett Fluckey was an energetic and curious ten-year-old. Due to his likable nature, he was blessed with many friends. People noticed his engaging smile, his red hair, and his face full of freckles. He once won a "freckles contest" and always claimed to have won a "smile contest," too. He enjoyed a wide range of interests, from sports to science, as well as scouting, where he excelled and eventually earned the rank of Eagle Scout.

What the young Fluckey was not, though, was a good student. His teachers shared with his parents that they thought he was exceptionally bright. He simply refused to apply himself to his classwork. That was disappointing to Isaac Newton Fluckey and Louella Snowden Fluckey. His dad, Newt Fluckey, was especially agitated by the reports he was getting. He and his wife believed strongly in education and pushed learning and academic achievement to their four children, Jim, Ken, Eugene, and Lucy. Newt was obsessed with the idea of each of them eventually earning admission to one specific college: Princeton University. At least the three boys. Females were not yet allowed at the school. He was convinced that Princeton and the Ivy League represented the epitome of academia. That and his offspring's best opportunities for success in life. Certainly better than what the elder Fluckey had achieved.

This dream of Princeton for the boys came despite the family's limited finances. They were not poor, but the children would have to rely on scholarships and work if they had any hope of fulfilling their father's ambitions.

Still, young Gene was interested in what he was interested in. He preferred to go his own way. His love for science and engineering had led him to build a simple crystal radio set and he would spend hours seeing what distant signals he could intercept from his bedroom in Washington, DC.

One night, he pulled in a station from Pittsburgh, Pennsylvania, that was broadcasting a speech by the country's new president, Calvin Coolidge. Coolidge had been elected vice president in 1920, on the ticket with Warren G. Harding. It was the first election in history in which voting returns were broadcast live on the new medium of radio. Then Coolidge abruptly became president when Harding died of a heart attack in August of 1923.

Normally, the boy would have tweaked his crystal set and tried to find another, more distant station. Not this night. The speech the president was giving resonated with Gene. He was so impressed with Coolidge's advice that he wrote down every word so he could remember it later.

The man many called Silent Cal was not known for inspiring speeches. Some writers had joked that Coolidge was "silent in five languages." Another, describing the new president's dour demeanor, said he appeared to have been "weaned on a pickle." However, Coolidge's speech that evening spoke volumes to a redheaded kid named Eugene Fluckey.

The words that would guide the boy for the rest of his life were "Nothing in the world can take the place of persistence. Talent will not; nothing is more common than unsuccessful men with talent. Genius will not; unrewarded genius is almost a proverb. Education will not; the world is full of educated derelicts. Persistence and determination alone are omnipotent. The slogan Press On! has solved and always will solve the problems of the human race."

Gene was so inspired by those words that he promptly named his new puppy Calvin Coolidge. As further evidence of just how much the boy was influenced by the speech, he immediately became more persistent in his schoolwork, dramatically improved his grades, completed elementary school the next year ahead of schedule, and graduated from Western High School at the age of fifteen.

Fluckey was born in Washington, DC, on October 5, 1913, the third of the four children. His parents had moved to the nation's capital from Illinois so his father could work as a paralegal at the Justice Department. Newt Fluckey soon enrolled in law school and would eventually become a lawyer in that office. But despite his excellent effort and sheer volume of work cleared, he seemed to never earn a promotion. Years later, he would learn he had been denied advancement because he made those for whom he worked look better. They could not afford to move him up. That frustration was just one reason Fluckey wanted his children to get a better education than he had received. And Princeton was the place he was convinced would afford them that leg up.

That was why, when Eugene finished high school at such an early age, too young to be accepted and begin studies at Princeton, Newt and Louella sacrificed and scrimped to be able to send their precocious son to Mercersburg Academy. That was a respected and expensive college preparatory school, in business in Mercersburg, Pennsylvania, since 1836. By all accounts, the boy's determination to persist and press on continued there. He excelled.

However, the road to the Ivy League would soon take a literal hard right turn, thanks in part to a next-door neighbor of the Fluckeys. Adolphus Staton was a US Navy hero, the recipient of the Medal of Honor for action at the port of Veracruz in 1914, then the Navy Cross for helping save the ship on which he was serving when the vessel was torpedoed during World War I. Staton also happened to be a graduate of the US Naval Academy in Annapolis, class of 1902.

When Captain Staton learned that the kid next door had an interest not only in science, sports, and engineering but also in military history, he strongly suggested that the boy consider the Academy, then a career as an officer in the Navy. Eugene enthusiastically took to the notion, much to the consternation of his father. But then, for financial and other reasons, Newt warmed to the idea. Captain Staton suggested the boy attend Columbian Preparatory School in Washington, DC. The institution specialized in helping applicants to the service academies get the highest scores possible on their entrance exams to enhance their chances of being sponsored and admitted.

The former mediocre student did just fine there, too, finishing first in his class and excelling on his SAT tests, including in subject areas attractive to the Naval Academy. But there was a new problem. Because of the Great Depression, and with millions out of work, many young men were attracted to the free college education and promise of military careers offered by West Point, the Coast Guard Academy, and Annapolis. Even with his dad's connections in government, Gene and his parents were unable to find a member of Congress who had not already filled his quota of nomination candidates. At the last minute, Newt contacted the representative in Congress from his old district back in Illinois. As it happened, one of the young men the congressman had sponsored had declined the appointment. He agreed to add young Fluckey to his list.

Perseverance had paid off. Gene entered the Naval Academy in June of 1931.

The structure and demands of the service academy fit Fluckey perfectly. He excelled in his classes and honed his leadership skills. He also participated in rowing, wrestling, and football. But then, as he entered his third year, there was another considerable challenge.

Every midshipman at the Academy had to take a physical to be certain he qualified to advance. Those who failed any portion of the medical exam would be allowed to complete what was the equivalent of their junior year of college. However, they would then have to submit their resignations and leave the Academy without a degree and forfeit becoming an officer.

Fluckey had no concerns. He was in top shape and the best of health.

But then came the eye exam. Gene discovered that he had severe myopia. Twenty/twenty vision without corrective lenses was a requirement for all to continue in and graduate from the Academy. He was 11/20.

Another opportunity to persevere. He studied the situation and came up with a self-prescribed means to try to overcome the problem. He decided the vision issue was the result of spending so much time devouring books, something he had done since he first learned how, as well as all the reading he had done in preparation for entering the Academy. That, he theorized, had distorted the muscles in his eyes. There should be a way to re-train those muscles to get him back to 20/20.

Eye doctors he consulted about his hypothesis disagreed. But it made sense to Fluckey and he pressed on.

He prescribed himself three lenses of different intensity—mild, average, and strong—with the intention of alternating their use while reading. But no optician would fill scrips written by a college student, not even a student from Annapolis. Finally, his father talked with a friend who was an eye surgeon. The doctor agreed to meet with Gene and hear his ideas. Though the doctor doubted it would ever work, he was impressed with the young man's persistence. Besides, there was no harm in trying. He went ahead and wrote the orders for the three lenses.

At first, Gene's "eye exercises" did not seem to be making any difference at all. In the beginning, his eyesight got worse, but he did not give up.

Then, only a few days before the results of his physical would be finalized and he would be asked to resign from Annapolis, he approached the examiners to give him another chance to pass the eye test. They refused. There was no point. He had a serious vision issue. Eyesight issues such as Fluckey's did not improve so remarkably in only a few months.

Again, Fluckey persisted. The examiner ultimately relented, just to get rid of the pesky midshipman. When he was finally tested, Fluckey amazed the examiner by being able to read the bottom line of the eye chart. The examiner assumed Gene had somehow memorized the letters. He pulled out five more charts, all new and never used. Fluckey was able to read all of them equally well.

Gene's perseverance had allowed him to overcome a seemingly insurmountable obstacle yet again. He was on his way to his final year at the Academy and his commissioning as an ensign in the US Navy. However, he had no way of knowing that he would soon face yet another powerful hurdle he would have to overcome.

His mother, Louella Fluckey, was an accomplished, talented artist. However, she had placed her own aspirations on hold to assist her husband in assuring their children had all they needed to pursue their education. To supplement the family's income, she painted scenes on china plates and cups and sold them to stores in the area. She also gave art lessons and took boarders into their home. Louella took great pride in the accomplishments of their children. She was especially gratified by Gene and his decision to go to the Naval Academy. Though her husband may not have agreed, she felt there was more honor and prestige in her boy becoming a naval officer than in earning a degree at Princeton.

In June of 1934, she and Newt drove down to Norfolk, Virginia, to see their son off on his midshipman summer cruise. Eugene's previous summer cruise, between his sophomore and junior year, had been something of a dud. The Navy had experienced severe budget cutbacks since the Great War had ended. That summer's trip had not been to exotic overseas locations, as was typical. Instead, they had traveled along the US coast and into the Gulf of Mexico, down to Houston, Texas, and back. The future naval officers had mostly scraped paint and done manual labor for more than two months at sea. Even though Eugene maintained he had learned a great deal about seamanship and naval engineering, he was looking forward to the '34 cruise. They were to travel aboard the battleship USS *Wyoming* (BB-32), and this year they were headed across the Atlantic, for England and the Mediterranean Sea.

Though they hated to see him gone from home for such a long time, Newt and Louella Fluckey were excited for the experiences he would have. They also understood that he would be judged on his performance on the cruise. That would play a major role in the balance of his time at the Academy and beyond.

On the way back home to Washington, DC, that day, after seeing Gene off, his parents were involved in a serious automobile accident. Their vehicle was struck by a drunk driver. Newt and Louella survived the crash but were both seriously hurt. Even so, not wanting to interrupt their son's cruise or distract him in any way, they did not even let him know about their wreck or the severity of their injuries. There was nothing he could do about it anyway.

Indeed, Eugene was having a fine voyage, learning a great deal, visiting exotic locations, and meeting many famous people. The midshipmen had dinner in London with actor Douglas Fairbanks Jr.—who would later serve as a decorated naval officer in World War II—had an audience with Pope Pius XI in the Vatican, met briefly with Italian dictator Benito Mussolini and gave him a rousing US Navy cheer, and even had President Franklin Roosevelt visit them once they returned to the States and were conducting drills at the mouth of the Potomac River.

While Gene was away, though, Louella developed complications from her injuries. She was in critical condition, on the verge of death. At that point, Newt did send a letter to Gene, telling his son not to interrupt the trip but to pray for his mother's recovery. He knew how very important it was for his son to complete this last major cruise before graduation. Cutting it short could jeopardize everything.

Gene was devastated. He considered leaving the cruise, heading for home, but his father was very adamant in his letter that he not do so.

The next letter Gene received was from his sister, Lucy. His mother had passed away. But Lucy, too, made sure Eugene knew that Louella would not have wanted him to risk his career just to show up at her funeral.

Again, Fluckey was torn. But once again he made the heart-rending decision to remain with the *Wyoming* and his fellow midshipmen. That was a choice that would nag him for the rest of his days. Especially when he would later have to leave his wife, who had significant medical issues, for months at a time while he served his country.

There was one good omen near the completion of that summer cruise, though. As the *Wyoming* was approaching Norfolk on their return, Fluckey looked out ahead of the bow of the battleship and he could see a pod of dolphins frolicking in the dark blue Atlantic waters. They appeared to be leading the way to port. In seafaring lore, dolphins signify good luck.

Though he did not know it then, the young man would one day wear a dolphin pin on his shirt, and he would bear the nickname Lucky Fluckey.

Deservedly so.

★ CHAPTER TWO ★

"ELIMINATION OF RED TAPE"

"On 16 May 1945 departed Navy Yard for Pearl Harbor. Voyage repairs at Pearl Harbor accomplished by SubRon 18 and U.S.S. EURYALE, very cooperative and very good. Readiness for sea date 8 June 1945. Installed rocket launcher. Cmdr. H. HULL co-suggested. Admire his elimination of red tape to procure it."

—From "Report of Twelfth War Patrol," USS *Barb* (SS-220)

Commander Eugene B. Fluckey was more aware than most that not every battle could be won. The object was to win more than you lost, to live to fight again, and, hopefully, to win the next one. Despite his lobbying, he had reluctantly agreed to accept his Medal of Honor. The ceremony took place in the office of Secretary of the Navy James Forrestal in Washington, DC, on March 23, 1945. Fluckey's wife, Marjorie, was by his side. Young daughter Barbara was allowed to remain in school since it was her last day there. Fluckey and Marjorie had stopped by his dad's apartment to see if he felt like attending the event with them. Newt Fluckey politely declined but asked that they stop by again afterward if they had time. He had never seen a Medal of Honor in person before.

The newspapers in Washington made the ceremony a front-page feature. There were large photos of Fluckey, Marjorie, Forrestal, and the chef of naval operations, Fleet Admiral Ernest King. After all, Fluckey was a hometown boy. This was exactly the type of news a war-weary readership loved to see: "Local Military Hero Strikes a Mighty Blow Against the Enemy in One of the War's Most Successful and Spectacular Submarine Patrols."

Admiral King shared with Fluckey that the president wanted to be present but was simply too ill. King also asked the honoree not to repeat that to anyone else. President Roosevelt was likely not going to make it much longer. Indeed, the president would die on April 12, less than three weeks later.

Fluckey would later have "Marjorie" engraved on the back of the medal. He maintained she had sacrificed so much that she deserved some credit for his earning it.

The day after the medal presentation, Gene, Marjorie, and Barbara loaded up the car and began a long, leisurely trip across the country. He would rejoin his submarine and crew at Mare Island, near San Francisco. Not only would the family have a chance to see the sights along the way, but they would have almost two months together before Gene took *Barb* back to war for the submarine's twelfth war patrol and his fifth as her commanding officer.

A fifth patrol that had been in jeopardy. But Fluckey had won that battle. Or at least was under the impression that he had.

By this time in World War II, the Pacific submarine commander, Admiral Charles Lockwood, had determined that his commanding officers needed time off after the trials of undersea warfare. Navy psychiatrists backed him up on this. From experience, they had all learned that sub commanders were more effective if they took a break after their fourth consecutive run. Bad things tended to happen to the boats when their captains became so physically and mentally exhausted. Not just bad things but deadly things—things that could cost a submarine and all the young men aboard their lives.

Plus, there was that thing about Medal of Honor recipients not being sent right back into the fray.

But, as was his nature, Fluckey persisted. As he sometimes did with his skippers—especially the most effective ones—Lockwood relented, despite his reservations.

The admiral had a reputation for not only listening to his commanders but for seeking out their opinions and input. After all, they were the ones peering through the periscope out there in dangerous waters, being depth-bombed and strafed. But he had been much less willing to give in to their pleas for a fifth or sixth run without adequate leave and rest. He knew how much stress they were under out there. He had on several occasions lost good men when he conceded, against his better judgment, and allowed them to make one too many war patrols.

One of those concessions involved Commander Dudley "Mush" Morton and USS Wahoo (SS-238). Morton was one of his most successful and colorful skippers, Wahoo one of the most effective submarines. Morton had convinced Lockwood to let him make one more run, even though Mush was clearly tired and ill. At that point, though, Lockwood needed every submarine skipper he could get. Morton was one of the best. Lockwood yielded.

Morton, Wahoo, and her crew were lost in October 1943 in La

Pérouse Strait, north of Hokkaido, the same waters that Gene Fluckey was now so persistently lobbying to visit on his fifth straight run.

Fluckey and *Barb* were scheduled to leave San Francisco Bay in mid-May 1945, bound first for Pearl Harbor, then Midway Atoll, and finally, if the CO got his oft-expressed wish, to the Sea of Okhotsk, Sakhalin Island, and the Kuril Islands. That area was all north of Hokkaido, Japan's northernmost Home Island.

There were reasons why Fluckey wanted to return to those specific waters. By the spring of 1945, submarine operations against the Japanese had become hit-or-miss. Boats were returning from patrol with few or no enemy ship sinkings to report. There simply were not that many good targets remaining in the usual shipping lanes out there. The US Navy's submarine force— never more than five percent of all warships in the Pacific— would, by the end of the war, be credited with sinking well over half of all Japanese shipping destroyed by Allied forces. They had been very successful in cutting the lifeline of natural resources headed toward the Home Islands of the Empire and the troop and supply ships bound for the far-flung territory still controlled by the enemy. That came at a cost, though: Almost a fourth of all Americans who served aboard submarines in World War II died. By the end of the war, fifty-two US boats would be lost and about 3,500 men killed.

Despite their effectiveness, innovative skippers like Gene Fluckey felt strongly that the capabilities of their unique warships were not being utilized. Now that he had confirmed with Lockwood that his fifth run was a go, he hoped to prove his ideas, not in a laboratory or on a test range, but in battle.

War inevitably leads to innovation. That was especially true of the submarine service. Prior to World War II, submarines were considered to be primarily defensive weapons. Not offensive. They were called fleet boats because their primary duty was seen as riding alongside the Navy's surface fleet, shielding those ships from attack, sometimes laying mines in harbors, used as lifeguards to rescue bomber crews shot down on raids, and patrolling the entrances to bays and harbors to keep interlopers out.

Otherwise, submarine captains were taught to remain hidden. Rely on their strongest asset—their stealth. Only launch torpedoes if there was an exceptionally good chance of hitting the target. Do not waste the precious torpedoes. Then, once the torpedoes were launched, they were to go deep, hide on the bottom, or, better still, run away. Take no chances. They were also expected to spend as much time as they could submerged, avoiding detection or attack from air or sea, only coming up to charge the electric batteries that turned their propellors. Then, as quickly as possible, they were to get back beneath the surface for safety. Never mind that the newer submarines could travel almost three times as fast on the surface as they could while submerged.

But when the war started, and with crucial elements of the Pacific Fleet on fire and sinking in Pearl Harbor, it fell to the submarines and aircraft carriers to take the battle to the Japanese. At least until more warships could be moved that way. Even then, with the US now also fighting Germany and Italy in Europe, the goal was to merely hold its own in the Pacific for the time being. America suddenly found itself in a different kind of war, and the Navy was ill-equipped to keep the Empire of Japan from redrawing the map of the Pacific Rim.

It is generally acknowledged that the Japanese made crucial mistakes in their surprise attack on Pearl Harbor in December 1941. They concentrated most of their bombs on the dreadnoughts berthed along "Battleship Row." Not only did they not hit the bulk of the massive fuel storage tanks on Ford Island or the critically important dry-dock repair facilities nearby, but they also failed to bomb the submarines that were tied up nearby or consider delaying the attack until the aircraft carriers based at Pearl were back in port from maneuvers.

It is also fortunate for the US that forward-thinking planners had already built some and planned more of a decidedly new kind of submarine, the *Gato*-class boat. They were able to dive deeper, go faster, and steam much farther than any previous submersible vessel. *Barb* was an early *Gato*-class submarine. They would prove to be exactly the kind of warship needed to fight the kind of conflict in which America abruptly found itself.

A new kind of submarine skipper came along, too, just in time to take advantage of this advanced war machine. In December 1941, the Navy did not have a single submarine captain who had taken a boat to war, none who had fired a torpedo in anger—but plenty who had been indoctrinated in the old ways of running a submarine. That is, remain hidden, fire only if destruction of the target is assured, then flee.

Some adapted. Many did not. Those who did not were replaced, one by one, by commanders who were more aggressive, who pushed the *Gato* boats to their maximum capability. Then their even more advanced successors, the *Balao*- and *Tench*-class submarines that came along later in the war, pushed their crews and officers, too. These captains were willing to remain on the surface longer to take advantage of the speed and maneuverability they had there while keeping the battery charge topped off. They did not hesitate to use their deck guns—with which many skippers experimented—or to fire torpedoes while on the surface instead of only at periscope depth. And by being so assertive, they quickly struck major blows against the enemy and helped turn the tide of the war, if not necessarily in a very glamorous way. Most of their targets were tankers and freighters, carrying petroleum, rubber, ore, lumber, and other necessities— the required materials for waging war—from Japanese-held territory back to the Home Islands, or munitions and troops to occupied territory.

Submariners were charged with doing whatever they could to shorten the war. Severing those shipping lanes was a sure way to do it. Not a safe way, mind you. Most ships, including freighters and tankers, had guns mounted on their decks, carried depth bombs, and rode in convoys protected from Allied submarines by effective, deadly warships and aircraft.

Eugene Fluckey was one of those inventive and assertive submarine captains determined to push the limits. By May of 1945, he had already proved himself on his first four extraordinarily successful runs as CO of *Barb*. Now, if he could pull it off, he felt he had much more to prove. That stellar record gave him a leg up when it came time to convince his superiors to allow him to have his way.

While at Mare Island for refit, the *Barb* had been equipped with a five-inch deck gun aft of the conning tower. That replaced the four-inch gun that had been mounted forward of the conning tower. Fluckey had made that request so he would have a weapon that packed a bit more wallop, but also one that he could use should they find themselves being chased while on the surface, which had happened on one of his previous patrols on *Barb*.

The boat had also had the newly developed ST radar installed. This periscope-mounted system allowed the submarine to "see" ships and aircraft in the area better and provide range and bearing with more accuracy. Previously, there was much guesswork involved, with only the periscope to provide a view of the target. Sonar could give more data, but it emitted an audible ping that could be heard by the vessel being stalked. The Japanese had no way to detect this new type of silent and highly effective radar.

There were other changes. Two officers were transferred off *Barb* and two more came aboard. Fifteen sailors were transferred. That was almost a quarter of her complement of crewmembers. That was commonplace by this time: attempting to keep a mix of experienced sailors to match up with newcomers fresh out of submarine school.

Now, as *Barb* prepared to get underway, Fluckey had plans for that space on her deck that had been vacated by the four-inch gun. He wanted to install a rocket launcher there. He had begun making arrangements to do just that once they arrived at Pearl Harbor: take on board a hundred Mark 10 rockets. He already knew the target that would allow him to prove the effectiveness of using a submarine as a launch platform for a ballistic missile. Fluckey would later describe his intent as "creating maximum harassment with minimum force."

Spirits were high among the crew as *Barb* departed Mare Island and San Francisco on May 16, 1945. Not only had they just completed one of the most successful patrols of the war, but their captain had been awarded the Medal of Honor. Few submariners had been so honored. The officers and men of *Barb* were proud their skipper was one of them. There was also the wonderful news out of Europe that gave everybody hope. Only a week before, on Tuesday, May 8, the Allies had accepted Germany's unconditional surrender. The war in Europe was over. Surely Japan would not be able to last much longer without Hitler still in the fight. Maybe, with the pressure off on its western front, the Russians would finally enter the war against Japan, as they had been promising to do.

But the men well knew that the Empire of Japan had vowed to fight to the last man, woman, and child, and promised that any attempt to invade the Home Islands would result in millions of lives lost. It would never succeed, the Japanese maintained. No such assault ever had. Not throughout the Empire's long history.

There may have been hopeful signs that the war was winding down, but those were still treacherous waters to which *Barb* was steaming. It had also been yet another painful parting for Gene and Marjorie and their daughter, with no idea of when they would be reunited.

Once the *Barb* docked in Hawaii, Fluckey's first stop was at the office of Commander Harry Hull, a gunnery officer on the staff of the Pacific Submarine Commander. Fluckey had already been in touch with Hull, an old friend, and had explained his reasoning about becoming the first submarine in history to be armed with rockets. Hull was in a position to make it happen, and make sure such a launcher and rockets were available for *Barb* when she arrived in Hawaii on May 24. Or at least by the time she was ready to leave, heading westward on patrol.

But first, Fluckey assumed he would need to sell Hull on the idea. For that, he resorted to skills honed back during his summers when, as a teenager, he sold brushes door-to-door. With his patented smile and friendly demeanor, he quickly became the brush company's top salesman. His pitch worked on Commander Hull, who enthusiastically agreed to help him pull his plan together.

They would only have sixteen days in Pearl Harbor. Even then, most of that time the boat would be out of the harbor, conducting crew training or crawling with workers, busily undergoing voyage repairs. It was already a tight schedule. However, Harry Hull, once he was sold on the idea, was busily getting everything done before *Barb* and her crew steamed back to the war.

The launcher Fluckey had settled on was available on Oahu, but it was being used in some important testing elsewhere on the island. Hull was confident that he could grab it and also obtain a hundred Mark 10 rockets and get them over to the sub pens in plenty of time to load and stow them in their limited space, and do so before *Barb* left for Midway, her interim stop.

Fluckey was elated. The scheme was coming together.

His next stop after his initial visit with Hull was the operations office. There he could get the final details for their patrol once they left Midway. It was always crucial that submarines be aware of which boats were operating where to avoid running into each other. Fluckey felt this visit was to be little more than a formality. Admiral Lockwood had approved it already: *Barb* was bound for the Sea of Okhotsk, the site of her eighth run and Fluckey's first as her CO.

When he walked in the door of the operations office, though, he was blindsided. There had been a major change in plans for the hero and his now-famous submarine.

Barb was now assigned to perform lifeguard duty off Wake Island. That would put them more than two thousand miles from the Kuriles and that target at which Fluckey planned to aim his new five-inch, high-capacity, spin-stabilized rockets. The spot where he had already promised his commanders that he would do more than a million dollars' worth of damage and, most important, demonstrate yet another new and exciting capability for submarines.

The operations officer said he assumed the reassignment was due to the Medal of Honor tradition. The officer was not moved, either, when Fluckey explained that Charlie Lockwood himself had promised *Barb* a patrol in the Sea of Okhotsk and the Kuriles, but the officer did share that Admiral Lockwood was due back in Hawaii in two days and he would make sure Fluckey could have an audience with him to plead his case. However, the man warned, the skipper should not expect any changes this late in the game.

Meanwhile, hedging his bets, Fluckey visited with another friend in the naval intelligence office, the home of the code breakers who had been so effectively deciphering messages from the Imperial Japanese Navy since before the war started. Fluckey knew that the Allies had been searching in vain for the remnants of the Japanese fleet, which had been hit hard by the Allies in several battles since the previous summer. The Navy suspected they were holed up somewhere, preparing to attempt to deflect the anticipated D-Day–like invasion of the Home Islands by the Allies. There was a good possibility those warships might be in the mostly uncharted waters north of Hokkaido, Fluckey contended. That was yet another reason *Barb* should go there and see what they could see, not swim leisurely around Wake Island, taking it easy.

That argument made perfect sense to the intelligence officer. Just like that, Gene Fluckey had another ally should he need one when he made his sales pitch to Lockwood.

When he finally sat down with the admiral, Lockwood admitted that he was not even aware that someone on his staff had countered the promise he had made to Fluckey. Lockwood had caught wind of the groundwork Fluckey had laid, lining up support not only for his rocket experiment but also his desire to steam to the Kuriles. The admiral simply shook his head and told Fluckey to ignore the lifeguard assignment to Wake but to be careful out there.

Finally, he told the skipper to get out of his office before the admiral changed his mind about the whole damn thing.

Fluckey was delighted. Unless the Imperial Japanese Navy somehow came up with a way to stop them, they would soon be on their way. Just to be certain, he dropped in on Harry Hull to check on the progress getting his rocket launcher and rockets aboard *Barb*.

"Gene, there is only that one launcher anywhere in the Hawaiian Islands" was the discouraging news. It was being employed at that very moment to test its possible use against kamikaze attacks, now a desperate but deadly tactic being used by the Japanese. The experiment for which the launcher was being used had become a major priority up and down the entire Allied chain of command.

"And they will not be finished with their testing for another three or four weeks. Sorry, Gene," Hull told him.

Fluckey did not accept the verdict. He convinced Hull to see what he could do about rushing the test. Hull promised to do what he could, but it would be tight, even if he could convince them to finish within two weeks. Meanwhile, always thinking positively, Fluckey got busy with the documentation Hull had given him, learning all he could about the launching device and the rockets it catapulted toward its targets.

He was especially excited to see they had a range of about three miles. Plenty enough for him and his "Barbarians," the nickname he had begun using for the *Barb* crew.

At the same time, he also studied old and unreliable charts of a place little known to most of the world. It was Patience Bay and Sakhalin Island, located at the southwestern corner of the Sea of Okhotsk, all very near Hokkaido. There was a potential target there, too, one that had caught his attention on the eighth patrol. At the moment, he had no idea how he might attempt to take it out. Maybe rockets. Maybe some other way. But it was another opportunity to show what submarines could do out there if someone only used his imagination and the inherent capabilities of these remarkable submarines.

Maximum harassment, minimum force.

Departure day from Hawaii—June 8, 1945—arrived. *Barb* was loaded, ready for sea and a five- or six-week patrol. But no rockets or a launcher had been delivered.

Harry Hull had continued to assure Fluckey they would be there. Then, early that morning, he reported that they had been loaded onto a boat and were on their way. The men doing the testing had worked sixteen-hour days to complete their job so *Barb* could have what they needed.

Still no rockets by early afternoon.

Harbor control was sending not-so-subtle messages that *Barb* had to get underway immediately. Their escort destroyer treading water outside the channel was growing impatient. They had other critical duties pending.

Finally, a heavily loaded vessel slid up beside the submarine and men quickly began unloading and stowing the rockets and launcher. An hour later, *Barb* was at last underway, down the channel and pointing out into the wide Pacific.

Fluckey was so happy to have gotten his new weapon, even at the last minute, that he did not consider the historic nature of the situation. Nor could he have envisioned that his experiment would one day lead to far more sophisticated submarines being primary launch platforms for much larger and deadlier missiles, thus providing a powerful deterrent to enemies.

"Captain, we got shorted!" one of the crew called up to the bridge. "We only got seventy-two missiles."

Fluckey, still in his favorite spot on the bridge of his submarine, and with a very big ocean stretching out before him, simply smiled and willed himself to relax. They would just have to make every one of those Roman candles count once they got the opportunity to shoot them off.

Fluckey was back in his element. In charge. Off to prove a point.

Now all they had to do was steam through enemy waters, make it to Patience Bay without getting bombed, torpedoed, depth-charged, or strafed, and, while on the way, figure out how to install that launcher on *Barb*'s foredeck and make it fire the rockets in the direction Gene Fluckey wanted them to go.

Press on, the CO told himself. Press on.

CHAPTER THREE

"AN EQUALLY GOOD OFFICER AND SHIPMATE"

June 6, 1935, was a bittersweet day for Gene Fluckey. He proudly graduated from the US Naval Academy—ranked academically at number 107 out of a class of 464 men—a member of the institution's Second Battalion. The next day he was formally commissioned as an ensign, an officer in the US Navy. But it was a sad day, too, because his mother would not be there to see him toss his hat into the air with the other midshipmen.

Other than just making the top quarter of his class, there was nothing especially remarkable about Gene's matriculation at the Academy. Nothing that would foretell the spectacular feats he would accomplish or the honors he would earn in service to his country over the next thirty-seven years—or his service to mankind beyond that.

At Annapolis, he was more attuned to his studies than to so-cial activities. Though he played football and other sports, he was not at the varsity level, nor did he excel at any of them. He still took pride in Navy's football team his senior year: They lost just one game and not only beat a powerhouse Notre Dame team but also edged their traditional rival, Army, by a score of three to nothing. (The star athlete who kicked the winning field goal for Navy in that glorious victory was a midshipman named Slade Cutter. He would one day be atop the same lists as Gene Fluckey as one of the best submarine skippers in World War II.)

As the Academy yearbook, *The Lucky Bag*, put it:

"Gene did not care to snake much because he wouldn't care to spend the whole evening with one drag, but his social life was well balanced by athletics; football, wrestling or crew always kept some athletic uniforms in the closet. Always ready to take half the table back on his side of the room when caught or to help push dust under rugs for inspection, Gene further quali-fied as an excellent roommate by his supply of good books and his readiness to make study hours more bearable by conversa-tion. For four years, he stood well despite the Executive Depart-ment and an abhorrence of textbooks. We see in him an equally good officer and shipmate."

"Snaking" and "drag" were slang terms associated with dating. Somewhere along the way, he acquired the nickname "Phantom."

The yearbook describes the goals of the Executive Depart-ment, which consists of faculty members who teach military discipline and officer leadership to the future naval leaders: "Be-fore giving commands, one must learn to receive them. Strict

discipline, sense of responsibility, obedience to orders, and coop-
eration are the essential fundamentals that this department
seeks to instill in the embryo Ensign."

We can assume Gene Fluckey was not that fond of strict military discipline, and that might later be a reason for seeking submarine duty, where the unique environment typically requires
such protocol be set aside. And his disdain for textbooks likely
came because he blamed his myopia in part on having spent so
much time with them during prep school and his first two years
at the Academy. At any rate, neither kept him from graduating
in good standing and in the top quarter of his class.

Fluckey's first assignment as a newly minted naval officer was
aboard the battleship USS *Nevada* (BB-36), by then a part of the
Pacific Fleet. The vessel had seen service in World War I, primarily escorting troop convoys from the US to England. The
ship was one of the escorts for President Woodrow Wilson's
ocean liner into port at Brest, France, in December 1919 as he
traveled there to take part in the Paris Peace Conference that
would eventually end the war, called "The War to End All Wars."
That hopeful description would not stand. More than twenty
years later, *Nevada* would be in Pearl Harbor on the morning of
December 7, 1941, tied up on Battleship Row when the Japanese
attacked, starting another war.

But Fluckey had moved on from *Nevada* well before then.
He transferred in May of 1936 to the destroyer USS *McCormick*
(DD-223), which was homeported in San Diego. It was there
that he met the young lady with whom he would fall in love.
Gene finally had an opportunity to snake and find a drag. He
had met a young blond-haired lady named Marjorie Palmer

Gould. He learned right away that she already had quite the sea-going history of her own.

Marjorie's parents were both British citizens who also spent a great deal of time in Providence, Rhode Island. That was where Marjorie had been born a US citizen in September 1914. Even as a toddler, she and her parents frequently traveled between Great Britain and the US. However, twice during World War I, the passenger liners on which they sailed had been torpedoed while crossing the North Atlantic. Fortunately, none of them was injured and they eventually made it safely to their destination each time.

Marjorie had other challenges growing up. While she was a child, it was discovered that she had diabetes. She became one of the first to be helped when purified insulin obtained from animals came into use for the treatment of the disorder in 1922. Because of her illness, she had been educated by private tutors.

There were other challenges. When Marjorie was fourteen, her parents divorced. She, her mother, and her sister moved to Los Angeles to live with an uncle. Meanwhile, her father suffered some economic setbacks and money became an issue. Because of her occasional diabetic reactions, no school would accept her. Without money for tutors, Marjorie became self-taught and helped support the family by becoming an accomplished seamstress.

A fellow ensign and friend from the Academy had met Marjorie at a reception and dance. He introduced her to Gene, who found her intriguing. He promptly fell in love with her. The day he first met her, Gene wrote his family to tell them to remember the name Marjorie Gould because she would one day be his wife.

But there were two snags the young couple would have to overcome. The Navy had a rule that any Academy graduate who married within two years of leaving Annapolis could be dismissed from the service. The regulation theoretically was to protect the newly minted graduate officer because his pay was not enough to support a wife and kids. Also, such hardship might endanger the investment the Navy had made in the officer. Fluckey suspected, though, that it was because new officers were shipped from one spot to another to prepare for leadership, which could create difficulty for a newly married couple, distracting the officer from what he really needed to be concentrating on.

The second problem was that Marjorie had been told that her diabetes would prevent her from becoming pregnant. She did not feel it was fair to marry with no chance of giving her husband a child. Fluckey convinced her that he was aware of the issue but that he wanted to make her his wife anyway.

Despite these concerns, and his being gone so much on the *McCormick*, the romance flourished. Gene and Marjorie were married in Long Beach—technically Los Angeles—in June of 1937, two years to the day after his graduation from the Academy. Less than a year later, in March 1938, diabetes or not, they had a lovely, healthy daughter, and named her Barbara Ann. Gene was at sea on the *McCormick* when he received a radio message informing him that he was a dad, and that mother and daughter were doing fine. Just off an eight-to-twelve watch, Fluckey woke up everybody on the ship to give them a cigar and share the good news. It would be almost three months before the destroyer returned to San Diego—only then could he finally hold his daughter for the first time. Such was the life of a Navy man.

That was about the time, June of 1938, that Fluckey became aware that *McCormick* was scheduled to be taken out of service and decommissioned in the fall. With a wife and daughter, he knew it was not only time to move on—that it was inevitable with his ship going into mothballs—but it was also time for Fluckey to consider what he really wanted to do in the Navy. Assuming he wanted to make it a long-term career. And he did.

After his four years as a midshipman at the Academy and three years on a battleship and a destroyer, the redhead was now certain about the direction he wanted to go.

Down.

———

The barb is a small, colorful, and highly active fish, but can become aggressive to other fish if placed in an aquarium without others of the same species. They are native to waters near Thailand and Malaysia. In many ways, the fish's disposition made it a logical name for a submarine. The Navy was, at the time, naming all new submarines for fish. In the summer of 1941, there just happened to be a sub under construction at Electric Boat Company in Groton, Connecticut. It would become the USS *Barb* and carry the hull number 220.

Many within the Navy were convinced another world war was inevitable. Hitler was ravaging Europe. The Japanese were gobbling up territory in China and around the Pacific while making threats against the United States if they dared consider blocking or sanctioning them. Even though there was little appetite in America for joining a war that did not directly threaten the US, many remained convinced war would soon break out.

Some in the military had strong opinions about what kind of fight it would be. Things had changed. It would not be limited to trench warfare or battleships blasting away at each other from a distance.

Technology had raised to a new level the ability to blow up things and kill people. Tanks and amphibious landing vehicles could enhance the effectiveness of mass beach assaults. Aircraft had come a long way since the 1920s. Warplanes now had a new way—aircraft carriers—of getting within striking range of their targets. Ever bigger carriers had become valuable as floating, movable airfields. But perhaps the biggest leap forward in military technology was the new generation of submarines, even if it was not nearly so obvious to the general public—or even to some in the Navy. With their stealth, firepower, diving-depth capability, battery life, fuel capacity, and range, they would certainly put a new face on the sea war.

Among them was a relatively new breed of submersible vessel—the *Gato*-class—that was moving quickly beyond the planning and drawing-board phases to become an imposing reality. And just in the nick of time. The lead boat in the class, the USS *Gato* (SS-212), was launched in August of 1941, only four months before Japan's attack on Pearl Harbor dragged a reluctant America into what suddenly became World War II.

The *Barb* was laid down—construction started—in June 1941, launched the following April, and placed into commission in July 1942. She was one of seventy-seven boats in her class to be built just prior to and during World War II. Of the fifty-two US submarines that would be lost during the war, twenty would be *Gato*-class boats.

But once she completed sea trials and was pronounced ready to go to war, *Barb* was sent in a totally different direction than most newly constructed submarines were going in those days. She became part of the newly created Submarine Squadron Fifty and steamed not to the Panama Canal and the Pacific theater, as did practically all of her sisters, but across the Atlantic, to Europe and North Africa. Her skipper was Lieutenant Commander John Randolph Waterman, who had placed the submarine into commission. He now steered her toward what would eventually be her first five war patrols.

British Prime Minister Winston Churchill had gone to President Roosevelt requesting that he dispatch submarines to help in the fight against Germany's notorious U-boats. Roosevelt agreed to do so, even when his top naval advisors recommended against it. Every submersible in the Navy was desperately needed in the Pacific, primarily to cut supply lines to the Japanese Home Islands and try to keep the Empire from expanding its territory or pushing eastward, toward the mainland of the US. The newer boats were especially suited for such a task.

Roosevelt prevailed, though. In general, since the attack on Pearl Harbor brought America into the war, the preference at the highest levels was to aggressively take the war to Germany while only attempting to sustain limited operations against the Japanese until the US could ramp up for a multifront conflict. Factories were gearing up dramatically and would soon be cranking out everything needed to fight a war. Troops were being trained across America. Meanwhile, it was mostly up to subs and carriers to oppose the Empire of Japan for the time being.

Not *Barb*. She became one of only a dozen or so submarines

to actively take part in the war in the Atlantic. Her first assignment was as part of Operation Torch, the Allied invasion of North Africa.

That assault turned out to be a nightmare. Some of the US submarines involved had serious issues with their German-designed engines, but *Barb*'s General Motors diesels performed just fine.

However, there were even more major problems facing Operation Torch. The waters in the area where the invasion was to take place were thick with U-boats. There was the constant fear that Vichy French submarines (French military units that were now loyal to and fighting for Germany) and other warships would rush to the area from nearby bases and overwhelm the invaders. Other Allied subs and ships were racing around with little coordination, complicating navigation. Amid all the chaos of the operation, one of the US submarines, USS *Gunnel* (SS-253), was shot at and bombed by an Allied plane. Fortunately, the boat suffered only minimal damage and no injuries. *Gunnel* was also one of the submarines that had been plagued by serious failures with their diesel engines. She was captained by Lieutenant Commander John S. McCain Jr., the father of John S. McCain III, who would later serve his country as a Naval Academy graduate, Navy aviator, presidential candidate, and US senator from Arizona.

Operation Torch would be the first major amphibious assault in history by US forces. All assets, including the submarines, were basically getting on-the-job training. *Barb*'s engineering officer, Lieutenant Everett Steinmetz, may have summed it up best when he wryly pronounced Operation Torch as "an ambitious undertaking that called for night landings by inexperienced troops launched from transports with insufficient training on a coast about which our forces had little intelligence." As it happened, *Barb* and her sister boats were unable to contribute much to the operation anyway.

After the experience off Africa, *Barb*'s first war patrol, they moved farther north for the balance of their time in the Atlantic. Hampered by highly restrictive rules of engagement, they were just as frustratingly ineffective patrolling the Bay of Biscay and other waters in the area as they had been off the African coast. During this time, they were based in Rosneath, Scotland. Among other constraints, they were not allowed to surface for any reason during daylight hours. If they spotted a German vessel in English waters, they were supposed to report it to the British immediately, then request permission before they could engage the potential target. There were also issues with so-called neutrality agreements with other countries in the region who were either aligned with Germany and Italy or had continued to observe a peaceful relationship with the Nazis. That theoretically meant that ships flying the flags of those countries should not be attacked, even if they were aiding Hitler and Mussolini in their efforts to gobble up most of the continent.

Barb's official record through her first five war patrols was not impressive at all. No sinkings. No damage done. They were not the only one. Not any of the subs in Squadron Fifty were officially credited with a kill. About the only shooting they did was at floating mines, and then only for target practice.

However, in actuality, *Barb* did sink one vessel. It would forever remain uncredited. Waterman and his crew were patrolling off the coast of Spain the day after Christmas, 1942, when they saw a ship that they were certain was a German tanker. Since they were in international waters, Captain Waterman called for a surface attack. It was nighttime and he was confident enough of what he was about to shoot at that he did not bother to ask for anyone's permission to do so. Two of their four torpedoes struck the target. It sank quickly. For the first time, the crew felt they had contributed something positive to the war effort.

When they returned to Rosneath, they learned they had some explaining to do. They had sunk a Spanish vessel. That violated neutrality rules of engagement, even if it was a tanker likely loaded with fuel for German tanks, submarines, and other war machines.

Waterman was ordered to deny they had surfaced at all, refute any claim that they had fired a torpedo, and certainly not admit that they had sunk a vessel. Meanwhile, British diplomats argued long and hard to try to convince the livid Spanish that it had not been a British submarine that had done the deed. In truth, it had not been, after all. The story was that it likely was a trigger-happy German U-boat that had mistakenly sunk the unfortunate ship of a friendly nation.

No credit for *Barb*, but no blame, either. Regardless, the capabilities of one fine warship were being sorely wasted.

Then, in July of 1943, things changed. The Navy finally won out over the politicians and the US submarine operations in the Atlantic, as limited as they were, came to an abrupt end. All boats involved were turned westward, toward home and new assignments, hopefully where the hunting would be much more productive.

Barb was summoned back to Submarine Base New London in Connecticut, arriving on July 24, 1943, and immediately began an overhaul. Then she steamed south, following the same route so many of her sister submarines had already done, down the Eastern Seaboard, between Hispaniola and Puerto Rico into the Caribbean Sea, then through the Panama Canal, and on to Pearl Harbor. Much of that path had been plagued by "friendly fire" incidents against American submarines. That was prompted by attempts to quell the German U-boats that were causing so much destruction and to protect the critical passageway between the Atlantic and Pacific Oceans provided by the Panama Canal.

But *Barb* made it safely. She arrived in Hawaii in September of '43.

However, her first patrol in the Pacific was disturbingly similar to what had happened while she plied European waters. It was not especially productive in that hemisphere, either.

But that, too, was about to change.

While *Barb* had been dodging U-boats and target-practicing at floating mines in the chilly waters around France, Spain, and Great Britain, a young, redheaded naval officer was learning his newly chosen trade, first at the Navy's submarine school in New London and then on duty aboard a couple of older boats.

He had begun contemplating ways to make these intentionally sinkable warships even more effective against the enemy.

Gene Fluckey could not wait to put those theories into real-world practice as skipper of his own submarine.

★ CHAPTER FOUR ★

"RAISE A RUMPUS"

GOOD LUCK BARB AND FLUCKEY X GOOD HUNTING AND GIVE THEM
HELL X HALSEY

—Radio message to USS *Barb* on her departure for her twelfth war
patrol, June 8, 1945, from Admiral William "Bull" Halsey,
Commander, Third Fleet, South Pacific Area

D uring their time at Mare Island and in Pearl Harbor, preparing for the boat's twelfth run and their captain's fifth,
Gene Fluckey had consistently preached humility to his
crew. He told them to not do so much bragging about the extraordinarily successful eleventh war patrol by the *Barb*. The
Navy and the press were doing plenty enough of that by the
time they left California, heading back to the war in June 1945.
Instead, the captain wanted to maintain an "all our submarines
are doing our best" attitude and not create any animosity toward him, his crew, or their boat. Though his admonitions had
lessened the boasting somewhat, he still knew many in the Silent Service had come to resent the attention and praise the
220-boat and her Medal of Honor hero skipper were garnering.

However, there did not appear to be any antipathy at all that morning in Pearl Harbor as they backed away from the sub base pier and got underway westbound. The area was filled with other submarine crews and support personnel, and they were all cheering, waving, enthusiastically wishing the men of the *Barb* good hunting and a safe run.

Then, as Fluckey and his crew negotiated the ship channel past carriers, battleships, and other vessels that were moored there, the crews of those ships lined their rails, waving and shouting their best wishes as well. They also sent bon voyage messages with signal lights and semaphore flags. Others sounded their whistles in salute.

The good-hunting radio message from the fleet commander, "Bull" Halsey, was the topper.

The tonnage sunk in the eleventh patrol had raised expectations for this run. Fluckey's obvious skill and daring tactics added to that. The sales job he had done on his bosses, convincing them to allow him a fifth straight patrol, only added to the hopes of all involved. The escort destroyer offered its own best-wishes salute and pulled away once they were about two miles out into the Pacific. Then, as the sub began its zigzag course toward Midway, Fluckey wondered for a moment if he could fulfill all that was expected of him and his crew. The bar had been set very high.

After all, pickings were slim out there these days. Subs were returning from patrols—even those captained by aces with glitzy records—with nothing at all to show for their efforts. Japanese ship targets had dwindled considerably. To find torpedo-worthy vessels to attack, boats had to penetrate the Sea of Japan, go right to the shores of the Empire or occupied China, and that remained downright dangerous. But Fluckey was convinced there were other targets that submarines could go find, attack, and take out. The rockets he had just taken on board would help him do just that.

The primary example he had in mind, and the reason he had been so determined to get the patrol area he wanted, was the telegraph cable relay station in the Kunashiri Strait in the Kuril Islands. Fluckey believed that if he could take that facility out of service, the enemy would have to resort to communicating via radio, where traffic could be easily intercepted. The code breakers could learn details of the movements of every Japanese ship in the region. Besides, as part of his sales pitch to Admiral Lockwood and others, he had promised to do a million dollars' worth of damage on this run. The telegraph station was, he figured, worth at least twice that.

Barb had spotted the potential target on their eighth patrol, but fog had twice prevented them from launching a surface gun attack. Fluckey also had doubts that his four-inch gun would have done enough damage to eliminate the station, but now he had the five-incher. And the rockets would provide the real firepower he needed for proof of a radical concept: that a target did not necessarily have to be seagoing to be worthy of the attention of a submarine.

Now Fluckey placed priority on learning how to use these new weapons he had pulled so many strings to obtain. Over the four days it took *Barb* to transit from Hawaii to Midway Atoll, mostly on the surface while keeping a keen eye out for enemy planes or ships, the crew practiced hastily setting up the launcher, loading the rockets, and firing them off. Since they had to be prudent with their limited supply, they learned quickly.

The biggest problem was that the bright, fiery tails of the rockets temporarily blinded the men on deck when launched at night. Any proposed attack would almost certainly take place in the darkness, since they would necessarily have to enter the enemy harbor and launch the weapons while on the surface. After experimenting with red-lensed goggles, they decided they needed some alternative way to preserve their night vision. They located some Polaroid goggles—glasses with special polarized lenses to protect their eyes against bright light—and put them on their darkest setting. They worked well.

Problem solved. Now, they only needed a real target instead of shooting at flying fish.

Barb moored at the busy sub base on Midway on June 12, topped off their fuel tanks with diesel, and picked up additional stores. They were underway again the next morning at 0900. According to their deck log, they were bound for their "patrol area consisting of North Coast HOKKAIDO, ANIWA WAN, and TARAIKA WAN, (Patience Bay) in KARAFUTO." (*Wan* is Japanese for "bay.")

Karafuto was the southernmost region of the large island of Sakhalin. That cold land had long been disputed, claimed by both Japan and Russia, as was other territory in the region. In 1945, it was occupied by Japan and was tactically important to the Empire, helping to prevent attacks by sea on the northern and western flanks of the Home Islands. The island was bordered on the north and east by the Sea of Okhotsk and on the west by the northern reaches of the Sea of Japan. The southern point of Sakhalin Island was separated from Hokkaido, the northern-most Japanese Home Island, by a mere twenty-five miles of rough but clear water known as La Pérouse Strait. Even though it offered direct sea access to prime Allied hunting waters, that passage from the Sea of Okhotsk and Pacific Ocean into the Sea of Japan was no longer being used by American warships or sub-marines by 1945. It was heavily mined, constantly patrolled by IJN warships, and was within range of shore battery emplace-ments on both the Hokkaido and Sakhalin sides of the strait. There were also air bases from which antisubmarine-warfare aircraft patrolled the pass. USS *Wahoo* had been the last US sub-marine to attempt to navigate La Pérouse, back in October of 1943. That legendary vessel now rested on the bottom of the strait, where her hulk often became snagged in the nets of local fishermen.

Now that *Barb* was back in these icy waters, almost exactly one year since her last visit, Fluckey intended to do more mean-ingful damage: not only hit unorthodox targets that he and the crew had spotted on that run, but inflict the usual mayhem with torpedoes and deck guns—and with those rockets, too. There were factories, mines, and railroads all along the coast-lines, especially in Karafuto, on Sakhalin northward into Pa-tience Bay. And now, after his visit with the intelligence guys and making it a reason for Lockwood to authorize his fifth run, Fluckey also hoped to locate elements of what remained of the Imperial Japanese Navy fleet.

14 JUNE 1945: *Crossed the International Date Line*

20 JUNE 1945:

  1200: *Position: Lat. 43-25 N, Long. 149-22 E.*

  2138: *Sighted ETOROFU ISLAND*

  2200: *Transited KUNASHIRI SUIDO*

  (*Suido* is Japanese for "waterway" or "strait.")

As *Barb* approached Etorofu Island, at the south end of the Kuriles chain, it was easy to recognize landmarks. Steam spewed from an active volcano there. Snow was still piled up along its slopes, even in the middle of June. *Barb* had arrived at their entranceway to the Sea of Okhotsk. There was also heightened anticipation because the narrow strait that would allow them to get into that body of water took them within sight of the telegraph station Fluckey was aiming to blast into oblivion.

They paused there for less than an hour waiting for darkness before beginning the transit between the islands of Etorofu and Kunashiri. The telegraph station was a tantalizing prospect when they drew near but Fluckey decided to wait. They had other things to do before announcing to the Imperial Japanese Navy that an American submarine equipped with rockets was in their midst. Besides, as they ran on the surface past the station, they saw it was once again socked in by the typical thick fog that blanketed these islands during their short, cool summer. Fluckey also knew from his past visit that the water got very shallow very quickly in that area, despite what their ancient official charts showed. The rockets were the best chance he had. They could not get close enough to effectively employ the deck gun. But all that could come later, after taking care of other priorities.

Then, while making their way between the two islands and reporting their position back to Pearl Harbor, they received a message that immediately changed all their plans anyway. It was from Admiral Lockwood and carried the "eyes only" designation. Those were the eyes of Gene Fluckey.

RAISE A RUMPUS AND DRAW ALL ANTISUBMA-RINE ATTENTION OFF LA PEROUSE STRAIT X HYDEMANS NINE HELLCATS WILL DEPART SEA OF JAPAN AND TRANSIT STRAIT ON THE SUR-FACE COMING HOME NIGHT OF TWENTY FOUR JUNE X LOCKWOOD X

Earl Hydeman was the skipper of the USS *Sea Dog* (SS-401). However, in May of 1945 he became designated commander of a nine-boat group of submarines, divided into three three-boat wolfpacks. Each boat was equipped with a new breed of sonar that was especially adept at detecting underwater mines. The mines had become a particular scourge for submarines as the boats more often searched bays and harbors for potential targets. Each of the boats had also been modified with what were being called cleaning wires. These cables were strung across the decks of the subs to the bow planes, the "wings" on the front sides of the boats that were used to control the angle of a dive or surface maneuver. The cables were designed to deflect the long vertical tethers attached to mines to hold them in place in the current. The idea was when a submerged vessel ran into one of those tethers, the cleaning wires would simply push it aside. That prevented the boat from getting snagged, dragging the mine down to the boat's hull, and exploding.

Some submarine skippers were opposed to calling these multi-boat patrols "wolfpacks." It was a tactic and descriptive term originated by the Germans and their U-boats. By this point in the war, though, as the number of targets dwindled, wolfpacks were now more useful and effective for American submarines. The efforts were enhanced by another recent development, the limited use of VHF radio transmissions to coordinate the maneuvering of the pack. The Japanese not only did not know about the use of frequencies above fifty megahertz but had no equipment capable of receiving such transmissions. The submarines could communicate with each other—on the surface—without worrying so much about breaking radio silence or being overheard by the enemy.

Admiral Charles Lockwood was so proud of this newly assembled wolfpack and the possibilities for them striking a significant blow against the enemy that he made a special request. Uncle Charlie asked for permission from Admiral Chester Nimitz, Commander in Chief, Pacific Fleet, to personally lead the group he had dubbed "Hellcats," riding along with them on their incursion into the Sea of Japan. Admiral Nimitz shut down that idea without even considering it.

For the two weeks prior to *Barb*'s arrival in the Kuriles, the Hellcats had been wreaking havoc along the western coastline of Japan. It would be considered one of the most successful submarine operations of the war. They claimed credit for sinking twenty-eight ships, many of them in previously safe harbors and bays along the coast of the Home Islands. Now it was time for the wolfpack to head home for fuel and more torpedoes, flying the banners announcing their achievements. The Japanese would be on high alert, fully aware these boats would have to exit the Sea of Japan. The Imperial Japanese Navy (IJN) diligently patrolled all routes the Hellcats might take to emerge back out into the Pacific Ocean.

Lockwood and Hydeman decided the La Pérouse Strait was the best choice for that escape, despite the estimate by Allied naval intelligence that nearly five hundred mines were suspended there. Most of them dangled at a depth of about forty feet, with tethers to the seafloor, perfect to snag vessels running submerged below them. The cleaning wires might prevent that, but the submarine force commanders decided not to chance it. They would make the transit on the surface at top speed on a moonless night. But they needed some kind of diversion going on at the time.

That was why *Barb* and her crew had been ordered to make as much smoke and noise as they could. They were to attract antisubmarine-warfare attention away from the fleeing Hellcats.

Though he did not need it, Gene Fluckey had extra incentive to help those sister submarines make it safely out of the Sea of Japan. The skipper of one of the Hellcat boats, the USS *Spadefish* (SS-411), was Commander William Germershausen. He had not only been Fluckey's good friend and classmate at Annapolis but also served and roomed with him on the battleship *Nevada*. He was also the person who introduced Gene to Marjorie Palmer

Gould and then acted as Fluckey's best man at the couple's wedding in Long Beach eight years before.

Another Academy classmate and friend, Commander Richard "Ozzie" Lynch, was the CO of USS *Skate* (SS-305), also a wolfpack member. Submariners made up a relatively small fraternity. Many of the officers on the boats had been Annapolis and sub school classmates, then served from the same home ports where they and their families socialized.

Unbeknownst to any of those involved at the time, from Lockwood on down, only eight Hellcats would be making their escape from the Sea of Japan on the night of June 24. One of the team members, USS *Bonefish* (SS-223), skippered by Commander Lawrence Edge, had built a stellar record in the war to that point. He had created havoc during this latest operation, too. However, *Bonefish* had been caught in the shallow water in Toyama Bay after sinking a large vessel there. The submarine was depth-charged and subsequently sank with all hands on June 18, 1945. *Bonefish* was the next-to-last of the fifty-two submarines lost during the war.

Her sister boats had no way of knowing her tragic fate, though, as they made their own escape. But as they prepared for the transit through the strait, *Bonefish* had not yet arrived. Any number of things could have delayed her, but she had not acknowledged any messages from anyone for six days now. Even so, the range for the VHF radios was limited and she could have issues with her HF radio. They could only hope that she was just over the horizon, steaming their way to join them.

Another of the Hellcats, USS *Tunny* (SS-282), received permission to linger in the Sea of Okhotsk, waiting for the tardy

Bonefish. But with no sign of her and no response to their radio messages, *Tunny* eventually followed the remaining members of the wolfpack making their way home. Those boats were able to safely negotiate La Pérouse Strait, thanks to the new sonar, radios, cleaning wires, and, of course, the skill and bravery of those crews and their commanding officers. Lynch and Germershausen—and each of the other Hellcat skippers, including Edge, posthumously— would receive the Navy Cross for their actions as a part of this historic operation.

But *Barb* and a couple of other boats helped, too, by doing as Admiral Lockwood requested.

They would go out there and raise a rumpus.

★ CHAPTER FIVE ★

BAD MOJO

30 SEPTEMBER, 1943

2230z Departed Pearl Harbor under escort of U.S.S.
ALLEN . . . and commenced passage to operating
area via Midway.

1 OCTOBER

0530z Parted company with escort.

I t took a while before *Barb* was ready for her sixth war patrol
in a new ocean. After their five patrols in the Atlantic, a
month at the submarine base in New London, Connecticut,
and the transit to Pearl Harbor, they spent almost all of September 1943 undergoing more refit and training. Lieutenant Commander John Waterman was an experienced submariner. He
had served in Panama from June 1937 to May 1940 as the captain
of the elderly USS *S-45* (SS-156), launched way back in 1923. She
was equipped with just four forward-facing torpedo tubes and
room on board to carry only twelve torpedoes. The boat could
safely dive to only about two hundred feet and was limited
to a speed of just over fourteen knots on the surface. Under

51

Waterman, *S-45* had only one job: patrolling the entrances to the invaluable Panama Canal, the only shortcut from the Atlantic to the Pacific. If war with Japan should occur, the canal would surely be a key target for the Imperial Japanese Navy.

When relieved from *S-45* in the spring of 1942, Waterman got orders to oversee final construction and sea trials and then escort the spanking-new *Barb* into battle. This was at a time when submarines and aircraft carriers were about America's only seagoing assets to stave off Japan's aggression in the Pacific. But, as it turned out, he and his boat went elsewhere.

However, as noted, there was nothing for Waterman and his crew to brag about on those first five runs in chilly European waters. They were forbidden to talk about or take pride in the only attack in which they had actually sunk a ship. Most would agree that it was a record more attributable to the submarine's hunting grounds and the restrictions on engagement than to any deficiencies in her crew, officers, or captain. But as a 1927 graduate of the Academy, Waterman was among those submarine skippers who had never taken a submersible to war or fired a torpedo at an enemy vessel. Also, in his previous command on *S-45*, he and his boat were involved exclusively in defensive duty, protecting the Panama Canal. That would make it difficult for him and most of his contemporary skippers to adapt.

Still, by all accounts, when *Barb* left Pearl Harbor on her sixth war patrol—her first in the Pacific—on September 30, 1943, John Waterman and her crew were upbeat and ready. After a two-day stop at Midway, she steamed on westward, bound for the coast of China beyond the island of Formosa. The first enemy vessel they saw was a passenger freighter escorted by two destroyers. The escorts protecting the ship indicated it was a worthy target. Waterman stalked them all night in terrible weather without an opportunity to line up for a decent shot. Finally, just before daylight, he felt they had a chance. They submerged and settled at periscope depth. He and his team quickly got into position, ready to fire two torpedoes from the bow tubes.

Then the three ships they were stalking abruptly zigzagged, almost as if they knew *Barb* was lined up on them. No point in wasting the two weapons on a desperation shot. That had been another between-the-wars dictum. Fire only if assured of a hit. Do not waste precious torpedoes or give away the submarine's presence on shots less likely to hit anything but the sea bottom once the weapons ran out of fuel. And besides, with daylight approaching, if she surfaced to try to angle for an attack, the escorts would be able to see *Barb* and come after her. No submarine would ever be able to catch the three ships while submerged.

Ultimately, all they could do was watch the potential targets disappear over the horizon. Soon Waterman could no longer make out the smoke from their stacks when he peered through the periscope.

A few days later, *Barb* spied an even more enticing quarry: a convoy made up of two freighters and at least four smaller vessels. But every time they surfaced and attempted to navigate to a point ahead of the targets, aircraft either popped up on radar or were spotted by lookouts in the shears (the housings for the two periscopes, radar antennas, and lookout platforms sticking up above the sub's bridge). With all the yoyoing up and down, the vessels inevitably steamed away from them until they, too, were well out of *Barb*'s reach.

There would be more potential targets. Three big transports, shielded by a destroyer and with enemy aircraft overhead, were running at high speed and zigzagging like crazy. Waterman could not manage to get the boat into an acceptable attack position, though not from a lack of trying. They were exasperated by the evasion tactics of the convoy.

Again, not even an attempt at a shot.

Finally, on November 9, they found success. On a rainy night, while running on the surface, they saw a radar blip of a vessel coming straight at them on a veritable collision course. When *Barb* dodged, Waterman could clearly see two ships steaming past. Radar revealed at least two more in the convoy. Once out of their path, the skipper could then see through his binoculars the two original vessels and at least four escorts. He had them dead to rights.

There was no time to dive, and even if there had been, they would almost certainly be left behind by the speedier convoy. In a surface attack, *Barb* quickly lined up and fired a spread of four torpedoes. Two of them struck one of the large ships with a blinding flash and a booming explosion everyone aboard the submarine could feel to his bones. Another fish hit one of the smaller ships, setting off a ripping detonation.

Barb had finally hit something they could talk about later! Long-suppressed cheers rang out up and down the length of the boat.

No time to celebrate. The escort destroyers immediately lit up the sub with powerful searchlights. They were already coming around, setting a course for revenge on their attacker. Waterman ordered a dive but as the klaxon sounded two warning peals, they did not get the bridge hatch cover closed in time. Torrents of seawater poured down into the boat, including onto the men in the conning tower. Then it flooded the control room, the heart of the boat, directly below the conning tower.

In the haste to dive and avoid the wrath of the destroyers, the submarine took too steep an angle downward. The flooding from the hatch and the steep dive sent them plummeting out of control into the depths. Somehow, a common maneuver they had practiced a hundred times had gone dangerously wrong. *Barb* was in even worse trouble than being stalked by enemy warships. Without some quick work to close and dog the hatch cover, and unless they could manipulate the dive planes and the effect of their dive tanks, the submarine was on its way to a collision with the bottom—or even worse, a depth where they would be crushed by the weight of seawater.

Once they got the hatch secured and managed to rein in their out-of-control dive, *Barb* had plunged to almost four hundred feet below the surface, nearly a hundred feet deeper than she was designed to tolerate. Their proudest moment so far in the war had suddenly turned into one of true terror and potential disaster.

But despite the portentous groaning and creaking of the boat's hull, and the awful tension experienced by the crew, the wild ride down to almost four hundred feet may have ultimately saved *Barb*. The enemy destroyers had quickly gotten to the spot in the ocean where they suspected the submarine would be hiding. The Japanese crew figured the American submarine would only be down to about a hundred feet or so by then, assuming a controlled dive was underway to no more than about two hundred feet. The destroyers began a vicious round of depth-charging, hurling barrels of explosives into the water and allowing them to sink down before they exploded at a predetermined depth of two hundred feet. As far as the destroyer crew knew, the blast would come just beneath the sub's belly, its most vulnerable spot. That would gut their adversary.

Without intending to be so deep, *Barb* was well below the enemy explosives. The rumbling blasts did little more than rattle the dishes in the sub's galley and maybe the nerves of a few crewmembers who had never experienced a real depth charge attack before.

The IJN destroyers eventually gave up and went back to pick up survivors of the two damaged ships. Once they got their breath, a few of *Barb*'s crewmembers were bold enough to whisper to each other the disparaging words they were convinced best described their submarine: "Problem boat."

From the patrol report for their sixth run:

DESCRIPTION: *Attack made on convoy by surface approach using radar with final bearings by TBT. Contact by radar. Seas extremely rough and very dark night.*

SHIP(S) SUNK: *8,000 ton unidentified AK**

SHIP(S) DAMAGED:

PROBABLY SUNK: *5624 ton similar to Meiyo Maru*

---

* *AK* denotes a cargo vessel. The Japanese word *maru* is attached to ship names and means "circle," indicating perfection or completeness.

With no other successful attacks to log and running low on diesel fuel and food (but not torpedoes—she still had twenty of them aboard and available for use), *Barb* returned to Midway. She arrived the day before Thanksgiving, 1943. It would be a while before they would have a chance to do better. From Midway, they were ordered to the boat's first visit to Mare Island, San Francisco Bay, California, for overhaul.

Waterman made it clear in his patrol report summation that *Barb* needed work. He even noted that the boat's main hydraulic systems were in such bad shape that they had almost caused the loss of the boat, including the dive just after their lone successful attack. There were many other defects, all recited in a full, typed, single-spaced page and a half of the report.

The CO was also worried about the mental state of the crew. Typically, by that time, submarine crewmembers who had made a patrol or two on one boat were being cycled off that one and onto another. That was primarily so they could mesh with all the new, inexperienced sailors coming in fresh from New London. But Waterman noted that many of his men had been aboard *Barb* for most or all of her six patrols. That, of course, included Waterman. It appeared the Navy had forgotten the sub and her crew had made five patrols on the other side of the world before her first run in the Pacific. And did not seem to recognize that the Atlantic runs, though not fruitful, had been no less stressful.

At least now the crew could finally brag about their "kill" in the East China Sea. Though they believed they had sunk two vessels, they would only claim the one they were sure had gone down, the first and larger of the two ships, the one they had observed sinking and clearly heard breaking apart, crushed by the pressure of seawater. Based on the patrol report for the run, *Barb* was initially awarded credit—and congratulated in the report's endorsements by various commanders all the way up to and including Admiral Lockwood—for one sinking, a vessel weighing eight thousand pounds, the unknown AK.

After the war, the Joint Army-Navy Assessment Committee (JANAC) reviewed all claimed targets sunk during the war and issued new counts. The committee relied heavily on Japanese naval records, despite their notorious inaccuracies. Almost all totals were reduced. *Barb* would have her one claimed sinking and its eight thousand pounds removed by JANAC. Her record to this day still shows zero kills on her sixth war patrol. No vessels sunk at all through her first six runs.

John Waterman and his crew had about a month to rest at Mare Island before they took *Barb* down San Francisco Bay, beneath the Golden Gate Bridge, and back out into the waters of the blue Pacific. They got everything repaired on the boat and had some new crewmembers come aboard, but Waterman did not get his promotion to squadron commander, as he had expected. He would remain at the helm of *Barb* as they zigzagged on the surface most of the way back to Pearl Harbor, arriving on February 15, 1944.

As was typical, there were new repairs to be made, including to the propellor, which had been damaged during the transit from the mainland. Also, the crew, including the newcomers, had to be trained on new gear and tactics.

By this point in the war, submarine captains and their squadron commanders were regularly experimenting, trying out some new methods to make better use of their boats. They also willingly shared what worked and what did not. The Navy would often make copies of patrol logs that the squadron commanders felt were especially enlightening. They made them available to other skippers to peruse and also sent batches of them to New London, Connecticut, where they would become part of the curriculum for prospective commanding officers (PCOs) at the sub school. Stopovers at Mare Island, Midway, and Pearl Harbor often included a few days to practice those new tactics so they could be put to good use during the upcoming patrols.

However, as the date approached for *Barb*'s departure from Pearl on her seventh run, her skipper was having some serious doubts about taking his crew back into harm's way. John Waterman had been at the helm of the 220-boat since the new submarine first started sea trials in Long Island Sound almost two years before. That tenure equaled the boat's entire life save for a couple of months' relief for one patrol back in the days when her home port was out of Scotland. While he, his great crew, and their submarine had survived some hairy situations together, they had little to show for the risks he had put his men through. "No runs, no hits, plenty of errors," as some of the squadron commanders put it. That lack of success was weighing heavily on *Barb*'s skipper by the time March 1944 rolled around and the next run was looming.

When they arrived back in Hawaii from Mare Island and the refit, Waterman was informed that this would finally be his last run as the commanding officer of *Barb*. He would now be in line for the expected promotion when they got back. Even if they returned with spectacular results from the run to the waters around Formosa, Guam, and Saipan, he would be bound for shore duty. They had no idea who his relief would be, but they would have somebody lined up to take command of the boat by the time *Barb* got back to Midway Atoll. Assuming they got back.

The more he thought about making this last run, the more Waterman was overcome by a powerful sense of dread, of almost palpable foreboding, a belief that a hex had been placed upon him and the submarine. And the more he thought about it, the more he persuaded himself that it could well be a fatal mistake if he were to take his boat out, as ordered, for what he and everyone else knew was his final run.

Despite his extensive experience—or perhaps due to it—he now believed his luck was about to run out. He could not tempt fate and place his submarine and its crew at risk. It would be his fault, he told himself, should they fail to return, regardless of how that end might happen.

Yet, if he told his commanders that he did not think he should go, his naval career would surely be over. Nobody wanted an officer who believed in hexes or refused duty because of nervous foreboding.

Only a few nights before they were due to take *Barb* back to the war, John Waterman made his move. Unable to sleep, he disregarded the clock. It was two a.m. as he left his quarters and walked over to the submarine tender USS *Sperry* (AS-12), berthed there in Pearl Harbor. He went aboard, found the cabin door he wanted, and knocked loudly.

He knew the man sleeping in that room, another submarine officer, one who had only recently been assigned the job of inspecting and overseeing repairs on some of the newer boats returning to Pearl Harbor from their latest patrols. Waterman knew of him from the days when both officers were serving in the Canal Zone, Waterman as the skipper of the old *S-45*, the other fellow as a junior officer on the equally ancient USS *S-42* (SS-153). He had convinced himself this man was just the person to counter bad mojo should Waterman decide to make that final run as the captain of the USS *Barb*.

That was why he was knocking on the cabin door of Gene Fluckey on a submarine tender in Pearl Harbor at two o'clock in the morning in late February 1944.

CHAPTER SIX

"NOT PROBLEMS, SOLUTIONS"

Eugene Bennett Fluckey settled on his decision to become a submariner for many of the same reasons other officers in the Navy had made that career move. Submarine service has always been volunteer duty. It remains so today. Nobody in the US Navy has ever been drafted into the submarine service.

When he went from his job on the battleship *Nevada*—with a crew of more than two thousand men—and shipped over to the destroyer *McCormick*—which featured a crew of about a hundred sailors and officers—Fluckey wrote to Marjorie that he was surprised at how much he preferred serving aboard the smaller vessel. He realized being on the destroyer offered a chance to perform and learn by doing a wider array of jobs. With a smaller crew, he could more easily learn the names of and get to better know each crewmember on the vessel. He could also discern for himself each man's strengths and weaknesses, which, especially in wartime, might be valuable knowledge in a tough situation. He also found the general atmosphere on the destroyer to be much less formal, far less military spit and polish. That was one of the few things he disliked at the Academy. From what he knew of submarines, Fluckey was convinced it would be even more relaxed on the "plunging boats." Submersibles of the time typically carried a crew of less than forty men.

He also believed that the Silent Service offered a quicker route to command of one's own ship than did most other vessels in the surface navy, and that was a top goal. He craved the opportunity to lead. Also, the crewmembers of submarines seemed to take on the personalities of their captains. That was appealing.

But there were a couple more reasons Fluckey applied for submarine school. With his fair complexion, he was continually getting sunburned on the decks of the ships on which he served, especially in the tropics. He figured that submarines would be submerged most of those bright, sunny days, more likely running on the surface at night. That alone would make life easier on the freckle-faced redhead.

And as a family man now, Fluckey needed the pay raise that came along with being in the submarine service. Way back in August of 1905, then-President Theodore Roosevelt took a two-hour ride in one of the early, primitive submarines, USS *Plunger* (SS-2). The sub was moored at Oyster Bay, New York, near the president's home. Roosevelt was so impressed with the crew and sufficiently unnerved by the experience that he declared submariners deserved combat pay, even in peacetime. Ever since, submariners have received more money than those with the same rating in the surface navy, up to fifty percent more pay while at sea.

The president (and former secretary of the navy), however, was not totally convinced of the value of the submersibles. Though Roosevelt told reporters he had thoroughly enjoyed his day, he also said, "I believe a good deal can be done with these submarines, although there is always the danger of people getting carried away with the idea and thinking that they can be of more use than they possibly could be."

Eugene Fluckey would have disagreed. He was certain they could be of tremendous use. He believed the submarine service attracted some of the best men, sailors and officers alike. He told friends and family that the submarine commanders he had met seemed to be a notch above other officers, both in intelligence and in quest of achievement. Men like Slade Cutter, the college football all-American, who had been in the same Annapolis graduating class with Fluckey. Cutter, who also served for a few years on a battleship, had already decided to go to submarines. He graduated from the six-month sub school just as Fluckey's class was getting started.

Such men had a dashing demeanor about them, an intense determination to take their ships to a fight, should one develop. Others had noticed. Sir Winston Churchill reportedly wrote, "Of all the branches of men in the forces there is none which shows more devotion and faces grimmer perils than the submariners." The author James Michener, in his book *Tales of the South Pacific*, noted: "I . . . saw the submariners, the way they stood aloof and silent, watching their pigboat with loving eyes . . . In the entire fleet they stand apart."

Eugene Fluckey admired that attitude. He knew it took unique individuals to serve aboard submersibles. They were inherently dangerous ships. Life could be uncomfortable and monotonous in what some derisively called sewer pipes or pigboats.

However, during his last voyage on the *McCormick*, Fluckey decided that for all these reasons, this was what he wanted to do in the Navy. Never mind he was further downsizing his ride considerably, from dreadnought to destroyer to plunging boat.

There was one more thing that factored into his decision. Submarine school would allow him to be with his family in New London for almost six months as he learned the trade. He could go home most nights to Marjorie and Barbara. That was the clincher.

Fluckey received his orders to New London while *McCormick* was in port at Pearl Harbor, on her return trip to California. He and his family would have precious little time to prepare for the cross-country move when he got back in San Diego. One important item was on the agenda. That was the christening ceremony for three-month-old Barbara. Immediately after that, the Fluckey family struck out for the East Coast. The christening and the departure for New London for their next big adventure were both on June 6, 1938. That just happened to be the third anniversary of Gene's graduation from the Naval Academy. It was also Gene's and Marjorie's first wedding anniversary.

They settled into a small house in the historic seaport town. But there was not even time for Fluckey to paint the baby's room or help Marjorie start her rose garden. School for Gene started almost immediately.

(The submarine base and sub school are actually located on

the east bank of the Thames River in the town of Groton. New London is on the west side of the river. Unlike their British counterparts, locals pronounce the name of their river not as "timz," but with the "th" and long *a*.)

Even for someone as bright as Fluckey, the coursework would prove to be challenging. Knowledgeable as he was about surface ships, submarines had become far more complicated as they also became more capable and lethal. Whether cook or captain, every crewmember was required to "qualify in submarines"—that is, to learn to perform practically any task at any duty station on the boat. This was based on the premise that, with a limited number of crewmen, if someone was unable to perform his job for any reason, anyone else on the boat should be able to step in and perform just as well. Practically any duty station on a submarine is crucial, especially while diving, surfacing, or attacking. Failure to do tasks correctly, or not knowing the proper procedure, could be disastrous.

From his first day on board a submarine, every sailor or officer began prepping for his "quals." By testing, he would have to demonstrate his understanding of all tasks and equipment on the boat. It was tough enough for sailors, but the requirements were even more challenging for officers. For either, failure to qualify within a prescribed amount of time meant immediate transfer to the surface navy. There, a mistake would be less likely to cause the loss of vessel and crew. Achieving qualification earned them the right to proudly wear the submariner's insignia, the twin dolphins. Those came—and still do—in silver for enlisted men, gold for officers.

The first order of business for Fluckey and the second class of

1938 at the submarine school was the physical tests, which were to assure the students could function in the trying environment in which they would soon find themselves. This included confirming adequate night vision to observe targets in the dark, withstanding high temperatures and oppressive atmospheric pressure, and swimming up from the bottom of a massive 150-foot, water-filled tower—thankfully, the water in the tower was steam-heated—to demonstrate their ability to escape from a submarine that might be trapped at that depth. At that time, if they were any deeper in a real emergency, there was little hope for rescue.

Fortunately for Fluckey, tolerance for the sun's rays was not a physical requirement for submarine command.

Classwork was highly technical, leaning heavily on mechanical engineering, diesel mechanics, communications, electrical circuitry, and typical submarine weaponry, primarily torpedoes. Most submarines of that time used huge diesel engines—nearly identical to train locomotive engines—to power the boat on the surface and to charge a massive bank of electrical storage batteries that propelled the vessel while submerged. The batteries also provided electricity for lighting, air conditioning, the coffee pot in the galley, and other necessities. Electrical and plumbing systems were complex but essential. Prospective submariners had to understand how to operate them and fix them if they malfunctioned, and do so under the most tense and chaotic conditions. At the least, they would likely be far from a tender or port should some vital system be damaged or quit working.

The study of submarine warfare tactics was an important subject area as well. However, the syllabus was based on little practical application. Nobody on the faculty had been to war in a sub. No active submarine skippers had, either. Nor did many of the instructors have real experience with the newer advanced fleet boats, the ones that would be replacing the older subs as soon as they could be built, launched, commissioned, and put into service.

Higher-ups in the US Navy had lobbied long and hard for more capable submersibles. Finally, a new type of boat, the *Gato* class, was being built, due to roll out in 1941. The impetus for their manufacture was provided by Japan's wide-ranging aggression around the Pacific Rim during the 1930s—that and the proven effectiveness of the long-range, deadly German U-boats.

Politicians and diplomats remained adamant about avoiding American involvement in another world war, regardless of the actions of Hitler in Europe and the Empire of Japan in the Pacific. But it was the position of some in the military to be prepared, just in case.

That same belief in the importance of submarines in a possible Pacific war placed even more emphasis on the New London submarine school classes of 1938. It would be important that these officers and sailors be prepared to take the helm or crew those new boats once they were afloat.

Of course, the sub school students were already putting considerable pressure on themselves. The long-established practice, as an incentive for students to do well, had been to send the bottom half of each graduating class to their first duty patrolling the Chinese coast in some truly ancient submarines. Families would not be able to accompany those who drew those assignments. They did not offer living quarters for families as other billets did. Most of the thirty officers in Fluckey's class were married. Competition for the top-fifteen graduation rank was intense.

Fluckey was disappointed in his eventual class rank: only seventh out of the thirty. But it was more than good enough to prevent his getting dispatched to the Far East and being half a planet away from Marjorie and Barbara Ann for an undetermined amount of time.

Instead, the new submarine officer drew an assignment to a place he knew well. He was bound for Panama, a spot he had visited often on both *Nevada* and *McCormick*. And, of course, his girls would be able to go with him.

Fluckey was to be a junior officer on one of the six S-boats assigned to guard the entrances to the Panama Canal. *S-42* had been operating for the two years prior, homeported at the gigantic naval base at Coco Solo on the Caribbean side of the isthmus of Panama, overlooking the canal's entrance and exit. The boat was already approaching fifteen years of service, having been launched in April of 1923. Though she was hardly as capable as the new boats would be—only four torpedo tubes at her bow, very limited in diving depth, and much slower on the surface— she would still serve as a good platform on which Gene Fluckey could learn even more about his newly chosen vessel.

The basics of how a submarine worked had not really changed much since the first diving boats: Flood tanks to dive. Use compressed air to blow out the water, increase buoyancy, and come to the surface. Use "planes," like aircraft wings, to control the angle and rate of the dive or surfacing. Propel the boat with one or two screws. Guide her on her course with a rudder. No matter how basic, though, these "simple" operations could be very, very dangerous.

Fluckey was excited and eager to take advantage of every opportunity to learn what he could about this interesting warship and its potential uses. And he was already thinking of new things he wanted to try once he commanded his own boat.

He hoped that would happen soon. Rumors were that with the big buildup in submarine construction in anticipation of a Pacific war there would be much demand for new, aggressive submarine captains, skippers who could take advantage of the capabilities of the new boats. Some were already calling the new subs the most advanced war machines in history.

There was another reason Fluckey hoped that command would come soon. *S-42* was constantly at sea, steaming around to the various ports in the Caribbean, gone from home port far more than he and Marjorie had anticipated when she and Barbara came down to Panama. He was not able to be with his wife and daughter nearly as much as he expected.

It seemed the sub was always at sea for holidays like Christmas or occasions like Barbara's birthday or their wedding anniversary, days that were important to the young couple.

It was not just that he missed his family. Gene had kept his promise to Marjorie's mother and sister and had assumed their role of helping his wife manage her diabetes. That was a difficult and time-consuming duty, but something Fluckey willingly accepted. Marjorie had written her mother that Gene had studied the disease extensively and that she was certain he knew more about it than her doctors—and far more than the Navy doctors. When in port, he was the one who kept her on schedule for her medication and was there should she have a low-sugar event, something that was still potentially fatal if not effectively managed. Commanding a boat of his own in New London would allow him more time in port to care for Marjorie.

In June of 1941, after more than two years on *S-42*, it appeared things would finally fall into place. Fluckey learned he had leave time coming; then he would be reassigned to New London. Marjorie and the baby went on to Connecticut to wait for Gene. The scuttlebutt was that he would be given command of his own submarine, likely one of the older boats, but that would not matter—being based in New London and skippering the older sub would assure he would be home more to be with and take care of Marjorie and the baby, yet it would still offer him the time to learn more of the intricacies of submarines. He was always looking to one goal: getting one of the newer boats and then doing spectacular things with the remarkable vessel.

Scuttlebutt was wrong.

Shortly after leaving Panama and reuniting with his young family back in Connecticut, Fluckey received his orders—but not to command. Instead, he was to return to Panama. He would be an officer on another older boat, one that had been retired and then brought out of mothballs back in 1937.

Everyone considered her to be a "problem boat," one crewed by some of the same sailors who originally commissioned her in 1926—some now in their sixties—because they were the only ones capable of making the unorthodox submarine function at all. A boat with a reputation as one of the worst and most dangerous subs remaining in the fleet. More than reputation. This boat had been so designated by the top echelon of the submarine force.

With Japan threatening, and with the Panama Canal surely a prime target if war should come, the US needed every asset she had down there—even a problem boat, doing what she could to help protect such a valuable waterway.

Fluckey was disappointed in not getting command of his own boat when it appeared so close, and dispirited about leaving his wife and daughter behind until he could once again find housing for them in Panama, especially since that was suddenly a very difficult thing to do as more and more naval personnel were being sent there. However, he did what he knew he was supposed to do: He pressed on and went right back to work.

His new ride was the USS *Bonita* (SS-165). He was designated as her diving and engineering officer. He had no idea in the beginning just how difficult diving and surfacing the vessel was going to be, nor how much engineering skill and luck would be required to keep the thing afloat and in motion without drowning everybody aboard.

One thing was for sure. Fluckey was about to have abundant opportunity to apply a maxim he so often quoted:

"We don't have problems, just solutions."

CHAPTER SEVEN

"SPLICE THE MAIN BRACE!"

21 JUNE 1945 Entered area.

Surface patrolling along northwest coast of KUNASHIRI

0015: CONTACT #1: Radar contact on two small craft at 4800 yards.

Gene Fluckey spent a frustrating June 6, 1945—the anniversary of his Annapolis graduation, his marriage to Marjorie, and the christening of his daughter—waiting for the delivery of the rockets and launcher to *Barb*. Finally, though, he could enjoy on June 8 the big send-off from Pearl for the submarine's twelfth patrol, Fluckey's fifth as CO. He and his crew still had a long run ahead of them. With the stopover at Midway, it had taken them almost two weeks to finally get on station. Or at least close. They were barely into the Sea of Okhotsk by midnight on June 21. Now, at Admiral Lockwood's direct order, the submarine looked for any excuse to shoot at something so as to create a diversion to have the Japanese come running to keep them from looking quite so diligently for the nine-boat Hellcat wolfpack.

Barb spent a portion of the long trip across the Pacific getting up to speed the fourteen members of the seventy-five-man crew who had not yet qualified in submarines. Fluckey hoped to have all non-quals tested and eligible for their dolphins by the completion of the run. He almost succeeded. All but two would make the grade by the time the patrol ended. The rest of the time was spent drilling, practicing, and drilling some more, all while keeping a watch out for enemy ships and planes. Fluckey had long since earned a reputation for remaining on the surface and running at a good speed in order to find targets. That meant the crew had to be especially proficient at spotting aircraft and enemy ships, then getting the submarine quickly below the surface if they proved to be a threat. And, as everyone had learned on the eleventh patrol, how to maneuver—often in water too shallow to dive the boat—to avoid enemy warships that came running their way after *Barb* unleashed considerable mayhem.

Fifteen minutes into the new day on June 21, 1945, they saw something of interest. They were not sure what the potential targets were. Not even when they got as close as a thousand yards. It was just too dark and murky.

Fluckey decided to wait until just before dawn to attack the unknown contacts. He and his executive officer, Jim Webster, went to their staterooms to catch a nap, leaving an 0230 wake-up call. They had already decided to conduct a surface attack, coming at the targets from the dark side, facing the rising sun, with any dawn light silhouetting whatever it was that they were shooting at, and they planned to use the forty-millimeter and five-inch deck guns, weapons of which Fluckey was quite proud. Only a few years before, deck guns on submarines were rarely used, an afterthought. The new generation of sub skippers found them quite effective, launching assaults, doing damage, saving precious torpedoes. Then, unlike surface gunboats, they could clear the decks and dive to relative safety.

The "Man battle stations, guns" call came at 0300, with a caution that everyone should be as quiet as possible, not even sounding the usual battle-stations alert gong. They started shooting about twenty minutes later at what was confirmed to be two "luggers," or multi-masted sailing vessels. They were almost certainly carrying valuable supplies as freight since each vessel was armed with its own thirty-seven-millimeter cannon. *Barb*'s deck gun crews made quick work of sinking them. Neither ship seemed to know exactly where their attacker was. At one point, they were firing their cannons in the opposite direction from where *Barb* floated on the surface, less than a thousand yards away.

All the shooting had awakened the locals on nearby Kunashiri Island, though. Lights flashed on along the coastline. For the moment, *Barb*'s job was to make noise and be seen. She had done that for certain, plus the sub already had two victims to tally for this run. The report in the patrol log noted that the first target "sank." The second was "a shambles." Job done, they raced away toward the southwest, on the surface at flank speed— about twenty-one knots—down the western coast of Kunashiri and toward Hokkaido.

Once the sun was up, they spent the rest of the day patrolling, mostly on the surface. As noted in the log, they were "not worried about being sighted since we have been asked to raise a rumpus." They did dive multiple times when aircraft got too close, and again when they spotted what they believed to be a submarine's periscope. They soon decided that it "was probably a seal." The skipper made certain, though, that they never submerged and then remained below the surface to avoid enemy aircraft for more than fifteen minutes or so. No way could they dash about and cause havoc in the region while underwater, where their speed was limited to only about nine knots.

While on the surface, Fluckey had one lookout watching for ships or periscopes on the water. Everybody else topside kept their binoculars on the sky, scanning for aircraft. After all, one sizable and quite busy Japanese air base was less than ten miles from them, onshore on Hokkaido.

While Fluckey was certain they had been spotted several times during daylight hours, they were only attacked once. An antisubmarine aircraft dropped two bombs close by. Too close. Fluckey would later say the blasts "reverberated like a bass drum on the hull." He took them down to below two hundred feet and set a course away from the area. They had gotten some notice, almost certainly convincing the enemy that an American wolfpack was operating just off northeastern Hokkaido. But now *Barb* needed to go elsewhere and pretend to be a different US Navy wolfpack raising hell. Fluckey had a plan on just the kind of hell he wanted to raise. He intended to launch an attack unlike any ever attempted by a submarine.

Fluckey called his leadership together for a meeting in the boat's wardroom, the compartment used by officers for dining and relaxing. For the first time, he shared with them the details of the eyes-only message regarding *Barb* redirecting the enemy away from the escaping Hellcats. He also told them what they would attempt before sunrise the next morning to create a very effective distraction.

22 JUNE 1945

> 0150: *Manned battle stations—rockets. Set up rocket launcher and loaded twelve five inch rockets. Set rocket range 5250 yards. Cleared decks.*
>
> 0233: *ROCKET ASSAULT #1*
>
> 0234: *ROCKETS AWAY!!!*
>
> *An inspiring sight.*

It was an order that had never been issued aboard a submarine: "Battle stations, rockets!"

Fluckey was about to prove his long-held theory that a submarine would make a wonderful platform for such an attack. They could sneak in close to shore, launch some hell, then race away, pull the plug, and disappear. He also felt the coastal town of Shari, on Hokkaido's northern coast, was a fine place to prove the concept. The city of about twenty thousand people had several factories, canneries, and sawmills. It was served by a rail line. Spurs off that railroad snaked into the nearby hills. That indicated there was mining activity there. The charts of Abashiri Bay, on which Shari lay, showed there were more than twenty fathoms of water close enough to shore to put *Barb* well within rocket range of the city's main factory complex. They could run on the surface but still have enough depth to dive and run if necessary. Mount Shari, a peak just beyond the city, towered to

almost a mile high. That would provide them a perfect navigation point of aim. The Nitoro Misaki Light on the west entrance
to the bay would also keep them in the desired area of the broad
cove.

Just prior to the attack, Fluckey issued two orders. The first
was "Quiet. Whispers only topside."

The second: "Control room, put four cases of beer in the cooler."

The launch of the dozen rockets—as Fluckey watched excit-
edly through Polaroid goggles from the bridge—only took five
seconds. The submarine was already ordered to two-thirds speed
and was moving away as the first of the weapons struck. That
was thirty seconds later. Everybody within miles of Shari was
about to be rudely awakened.

The patrol log described what those on the bridge of *Barb*
saw. "Rockets observed to fall in an area estimated at 500 yards
in diameter in the center of the town. Explosions were seen,
heard, and felt. No fires were started." Fluckey would later report observing chunks of debris being blown high into the predawn sky.

As they made their getaway, the *Barb* detected the activation
of enemy air-search radar. The Japanese assumed they had been
bombed by aircraft. So much for simulating a submarine wolfpack. Certainly, nobody would have suspected rockets raining
down, launched from the deck of a submarine. Still, explosions
in this mostly untouched corner of the Home Islands would create plenty of distraction for the Japanese.

Later in the day, *Barb* was well on her way to the southern tip
of Sakhalin Island and, eventually, into Patience Bay, northeast of
La Pérouse Strait. At 1100, Fluckey finally ordered a celebration of

the success of the previous night's assault. The order went out on the announce system: "All hands, splice the main brace!" That was an old nautical expression for commemorating some event or accomplishment by issuing the crew an alcoholic drink.

The men who were not on watch in other parts of the submarine gathered in the control room and spilled aft into the galley. There they enjoyed pieces of a huge cake the cooks had baked that depicted, in sugary frosting, *Barb*, the rockets, and the damage they had caused onshore. Each crewman also received a ration of "medicinal alcohol," sometimes called "torpedo medicine." In this case, the dose consisted of bottles of cold beer.

Everyone was in high spirits, excited by the success of their rocket attack. Just as the gala was breaking up, though, two reports reminded everyone that they were on a war patrol in dangerous waters.

First, the navigator informed them they had the southernmost tip of Japanese-controlled Sakhalin in sight. Next stop, Patience Bay.

Secondly, *Barb*'s radioman received a message warning that a Japanese "hunter killer" group—three frigates—had reportedly left the La Pérouse Strait area with orders to sweep the northern coast of Hokkaido. Apparently, *Barb*'s rocket attack had created some interest after all. The radio message ended with a single word of advice: "Careful."

Early the next morning, Fluckey once again sent his gun crews topside, even though the air temperature was near freezing, to get ready for a surface attack on a large two-masted trawler. A well-armed one, it sported one gun aft, one gun forward, and a large radio antenna. Fluckey knew this was a worthy target, and one that would likely inform the Imperial Japanese Navy that a submarine—or submarines—was, indeed, operating in the area, daring the enemy to launch a response. But the trawler would have to be allowed to make his report before he was inevitably sunk by *Barb*.

23 JUNE 1945

> 0423: *GUN ATTACK #2. Range 2000 yards. Commenced firing 40 mm at large two decked, two masted diesel wooden trawler similar to 150 ton class in identification manual. This is to determine extent of answering fire. First shot over, second short, third a hit. Expended three more rounds of 40 mm for 3 hits, then checked fire.*

The target ship was in deep trouble. Three more rounds, these from the five-inch deck gun, stopped her dead in the water as seven crewmembers ran about on the deck. They were apparently deciding if they were "content to be fried," as the skipper put it in the patrol log, or would instead dive into the icy water, where death would be just as sure but less painful.

Fluckey wanted to board the sinking vessel, maybe take a prisoner, and capture the latest sea charts for the area. But before they could do so, a huge fire erupted belowdecks on the ship and quickly spread throughout the vessel. The *Barb* had to move away in case something aboard exploded. Then, when the fire waned, to make certain the hulk would not remain afloat, they steered *Barb* past the vessel at a brisk sixteen knots. They sped by a mere ten feet away, sending a wake of water into a big shell hole in the trawler's hull. The poor vessel promptly began listing ominously. Then, filling with icy seawater, she sank.

In the process, one survivor jumped into the sea and swam toward *Barb*. Sailors on deck pulled him from the water. He received medical attention from the boat's corpsman for some serious wounds. While rescuing the Japanese sailor, crewmembers witnessed something they had never seen. Another survivor off the trawler, his decision made for him by his ship's sinking, was now in the water. Fully aware the men on the deck of the submarine were watching, the swimmer suddenly pulled out a large knife, showed it to the *Barb* sailors, and then slit his throat, killing himself, committing ritual suicide.

Fluckey knew he did not have room for—or men to keep watch over—prisoners of war. He ordered the submarine to patrol the area to see if they might happen upon other targets, and to continue to pretend to be a wolfpack. Ultimately, he brought *Barb* back to the scene of gun attack number two, the trawler. Fluckey told his crew that if the survivors had managed to cling to floating debris, they would offer water and food and direct them toward the nearest land.

> 0700: *After an hour's run returned to wreckage to see if the survivors had possibly made a raft. All had joined their ancestors.*

Next, Fluckey turned his attention farther north, deeper into Patience Bay. As he had told Charles Lockwood, he suspected elements of the IJN fleet might be hiding there, preparing to defend against the anticipated invasion of Japan by the Allies. It was as good a time as any to go take a look. The captain also wanted to watch for Russian ships that might be off-loading oil for the Japanese on Sakhalin.

Russia and her attitude toward the Japanese had been complicated. They had pointedly avoided declaring war so far, maintaining that they were occupied in a far more threatening conflict on their European side. That was true. They had eventually sent Hitler's troops—at least those that remained—fleeing back toward Germany. But even so, with the war in Europe now concluded, Russian leader Joseph Stalin still procrastinated. Russia would not declare war against Japan for another two months, until August of 1945. Fluckey heard intelligence reports that Russia was happily selling oil to the Japanese at huge profits now that shipping lanes from other sources were mostly severed. Since they were in the area, Fluckey wanted to see if that was true. He was not sure what he would do if he confirmed such trade, but, at the least, he could attack the Japanese oil off-loading and storage facilities.

They saw nothing. They steamed on up the coast.

Barb passed many factories to their west as they moved north, parallel to the island, in daylight. They made notes for possible future action against them. Now they were bound for waters near the city of Shikuka, which sat at the northern reaches of the half-moon-shaped Patience Bay. There, Fluckey was convinced, he would find plenty of potential targets. Some might even be cloistered but vulnerable warships.

Just after midnight on June 24, on an especially dark, freezing, foggy night, they approached the top of the bay on the surface.

They were dodging drift ice and taking constant soundings in these unfamiliar waters so near shore. The radar operator suddenly sang out, "Contact thirty-three thousand yards!" As they drew closer, the two radar pips separated into what appeared to be a couple of exceptionally large ships. Battleships? Aircraft carriers? No matter. Any large contact was also a large target.

There appeared to be no escorts, though. No destroyers shielding such delicious prey? How could they be so unsuspecting and careless if these really were big naval assets? Maybe even part of the main fleet?

At 0100, Fluckey had the boat at battle stations, lining up for a surface torpedo attack. They would first fire three fish from the forward tubes, then spin around and shoot two more from the stern tubes. The CO was on the bridge, directing the show, but so far, he had seen nothing but the two big targets reflecting back *Barb*'s radar signals as a couple of solid pips on the screen. Everyone topside spoke in whispers as they drew nearer to what they hoped were prime, unescorted enemy ships lying at anchor.

Seconds before firing the first volley of torpedoes from the forward tubes, and as they drew to a point just over two miles from the contacts, one of the lookouts suddenly yelled, "Breakers! Breakers!"

So much for whispering.

Fluckey was no longer whispering, either, when he ordered, "All back full!"—slamming a shuddering *Barb* into smoky reverse before she ran up onto a beach. Dry land. They still had ample water directly beneath them, but they were only yards away from catastrophe.

As they backed away, one of the other men on the bridge

peered intently through his binoculars. He casually reported, "Smokestacks. Factory smokestacks. We were lining up to attack a couple of smokestacks. I don't see any ships here."

Eugene Fluckey was about as embarrassed as he had ever been in his life. It was a sharp emotional drop from the elation of the successful rocket assault on Shari to the near torpedo attack on a couple of factory smokestacks, a target such a weapon could never reach.

The patrol log would not mention the smokestack attack. The entry would, instead, report cryptically, "Definitely no ships were present though pips resembled ships." But later, in his book about his time as skipper of *Barb*, Fluckey would confirm the whole fiasco.

Fluckey also told the crew that he intended to return to the city of Shikuka before this patrol was completed. Then they would get some manner of revenge for this bit of humiliation, most likely using the rockets.

They set a course for the opposite side of the bay but had to dodge seals and sea ice all the way. It made for a frustrating transit. They also found the shoreline barren, devoid of anything to hit with their rockets or anything else.

While *Barb* was lining up to torpedo a couple of inland factory smokestacks, Hydeman's Hellcats—at least all but one of them—safely transited La Pérouse on the surface on a freezing, foggy, moonless night and ran to the greater Pacific Ocean. That meant that *Barb* could now turn her attention to what brought her to these frigid waters in the first place: looking for the IJN fleet, sinking ships, and trying some daring new tactics, including another operation never attempted by a submarine.

Though her crew did not know it at the time, soon *Barb* would once again engage in some of the most intense action by a submarine in the entire war. It would be similar to what Fluckey and his crew had unleashed on the previous patrol, the boat's eleventh, the CO's fourth.

But this time, the furious clash would begin with a mysterious meteorological illusion, one that Eugene Fluckey would happily use to his own benefit.

But the outcome would be far less satisfying.

CHAPTER EIGHT

"THIRTY MINUTES LATER"

15 FEBRUARY 1944

Arrived Pearl Harbor. Assigned three days voyage repairs and seven days training . . . Dry docked to replace damaged propellor. Lieutenant Commander E. B. Fluckey, U.S.N., reported aboard for temporary duty as P.C.O.

USS *Barb* had long since established her own reputation as a problem boat. At a time when submarines were having plentiful success, her lack of production and near-tragic events on her first Pacific run solidified it. Happenings like the near-disastrous out-of-control dive on her just-completed sixth patrol that occurred as her crew was celebrating her only successful attack—not only of the run but the boat's entire tenure.

Then there had been an incident back in July of 1943 while *Barb* was still in New London for overhaul before heading to the Pacific. A sailor accused a warrant officer of molesting him as he slept in his bunk on the boat. When Robert McNitt, the newly named executive officer, confronted the warrant officer about the charge, he stormed out of the XO's stateroom, went belowdecks, and retrieved a pistol he had hidden there. The accused man took his own life in *Barb*'s pump room.

Another incident occurred as John Waterman and his crew nursed their banged-up submarine from Pearl Harbor to San Francisco Bay for her much-needed refit after that sixth patrol. Almost home, on a quiet sea, while running on the surface on a pleasant, sunny day, they were almost sunk, once by friendly fire, and then, as they attempted to evade that debacle, by another frenzied, uncontrolled dive. That occurrence did not show up in the skipper's summation report, either, but XO McNitt would later tell what happened.

A freighter appeared in the distance, but that was of no concern to the men on the submarine. Though officially still in enemy waters, even this close to the US, no one would expect any trouble from an obviously friendly freighter, most likely just out of San Francisco Bay.

Then, suddenly, the ship, apparently assuming the submarine was a Japanese I-boat, opened fire on *Barb* with a deck gun. As the first shells drew closer and closer to being on target, the diving officer ordered them to pull the plug and get below the surface in a hurry.

Again, the boat went under at too sharp an angle. McNitt would report the *Barb* sank like a rock. As they approached crush depth—the point where the pressure of the sea could destroy the boat—they had no choice but to blow the water out of all ballast tanks, using compressed air, in an emergency procedure. That sent the sub back up even more rapidly, in an uncontrolled dash toward the surface.

They popped out of the water bow first, at a sharp angle,

then crashed back down to settle amid the gentle waves at the surface. Such a thing is called a broach. And that left *Barb* on top of the water, a perfect target. Sure enough, the freighter once again opened fire. This time, when they once again dived, the crew was able to maintain control and avoided getting themselves shot or sunk.

McNitt, who had been gunnery officer on *Barb* while she was in the Atlantic, had openly questioned some of his skipper's tactics when speaking with fellow officers. He felt Waterman had been much too cautious, even to the point that it had gotten them into trouble at times. But McNitt also admitted he had no idea how he would run the boat himself in those situations, not as gunnery officer, not now as XO. This was how they were taught and ordered to conduct submarine warfare. It was not working. And it was threatening to get them all killed.

Those were reasons why John Waterman banged on Gene Fluckey's cabin door on the sub tender at two a.m. in February 1944.

Fluckey was fast asleep, still fatigued from the long trip from New London and Command School all the way out to Hawaii. He had only arrived the day before. His division commander had ordered Fluckey to the sub base at Pearl Harbor to temporary duty overseeing the repair of the newer fleet boats as they returned from their war patrols. There were two reasons for his being ordered to this job.

First was his record as something of an engineering wizard when it came to evaluating any issues with the submarines. He typically came up with ways not only to fix them but to make them better.

Secondly, the plan was to give Fluckey time to learn the *Gato* and *Balao* boats inside and out in preparation for giving him his first command, skipping the typical PCO's tenure as XO on another vessel. The plan was to send him out on a run as a prospective CO after a couple of months, riding with an experienced skipper. He could observe action and experience real-world submarine warfare.

As it happened, that early-morning knock on Fluckey's cabin door would speed up the planned process considerably.

Waterman sat down with a half-asleep Fluckey and laid out his quandary. He admitted he was spooked, that he was convinced *Barb* would never make it back from her seventh patrol if Waterman was CO. But he could not admit that to his superiors. He felt he still had plenty to offer the Navy, just not at the helm of a submarine.

Fluckey, of course, wanted more than anything to get combat duty and a sub command. He finally agreed to back Waterman's plan. Together, they would propose that Fluckey make *Barb*'s next run as PCO. Then Waterman would pull whatever strings he could to assure that Fluckey had command of the sub for subsequent patrols.

There was one other stipulation: It was a potential dealbreaker. Waterman wanted Fluckey to alternate night watches with him on his PCO run. Night was when things happened with wartime submarines. He was exhausted, physically and mentally. This was not typically how the prospective CO deal worked. The prospective captain generally remained in the background, observing, learning, but never actually commanding. On this one, Fluckey would be the CO on *Barb* about half the time. Two captains. Nobody knew how that might work.

Fluckey considered changing his mind. His first thought was that Waterman was pulling a fast one, trying to pass off much of his responsibility for running the boat onto someone else while he remained the CO.

But then Gene agreed to the entire plan, despite the unusual nature of Waterman's sharing of command. After all, it would make him a submarine skipper many months quicker than under his current deal.

When the division commander heard the pitch from Fluckey, his first reaction was negative. Despite the young lieutenant commander's high engineering and torpedo ratings, his bosses still wanted Fluckey to be more familiar with the submarines before getting command. But Fluckey convinced him he knew the *Barb* from bow to stern and proceeded to recite every duty station, the equipment located there, and how it was to be used in a variety of situations. He also reminded the commander of the current conventional wisdom, which said that most submarines that had been lost so far in the war had gone down on either their skippers' first or fifth patrols.

The first run was hazardous because of their inexperience, but every captain would necessarily have to have a first patrol. The fifth-run statistics were because the COs were depleted and fatigued from the pressure of taking a submarine and six or seven dozen men into war, enduring situations that put them under almost continuous and unimaginable stress. John Waterman was about to depart on his seventh patrol. The weight of the job was affecting him mightily. Fluckey did not mention Waterman's fatalistic attitude, but the division commander understood the argument perfectly. He saw the combat fatigue in his returning skippers all the time.

Seventeen boats had been lost in 1943. Already, in February 1944, USS *Scorpion* (SS-278) had not been heard from since January 5 and was presumed lost with all hands, likely while trying to traverse a newly laid minefield while entering the Yellow Sea.

Those losses included the most successful boat and skipper of the war to date, USS *Wahoo* and Dudley "Mush" Morton, in October. That had come only after Morton pleaded with Admiral Lockwood to allow him to go out one more time. Lockwood felt the legendary skipper needed a rest. But the Navy needed effective captains, too. He allowed Morton to make the ultimately fatal run.

Fluckey's sales pitch worked. The man who had as a kid won top-salesman awards and helped pay for some of his prep school tuition by selling brushes door-to-door had lost none of his skills. He later recounted the results of his meeting with his division commander in a letter to Marjorie, saying, "Thirty minutes later I was on *Barb*."

Fluckey would one day write about his division commander's words of surrender. He told the eager officer, "Gene, if you've got that many ants in your pants, get going. You'll get orders."

Such arrangements—a current CO, who likely possessed the typical skipper's ego, saddled with a prospective commanding officer with his own ideas of how to lead and how to run a submarine and how to win the war singlehandedly—would often create considerable tension. Especially when the current skipper was one of the old-line officers and the PCO one of the new, brash, assertive breed. And such tension was not confined to the wardroom, where the officers gathered, but usually spread up and down the 312-foot length of the boat. The sailors could not help but notice the dynamic and then worry if those conflicts might somehow put them and their ship at greater risk.

There is no evidence of any such tension during the first few weeks of *Barb*'s seventh war patrol. The "dual captains" experiment seemed to be working, but trouble was inevitable.

Barb would carry a very high-profile passenger along with them on the trip from Pearl Harbor to Midway. Mere moments before departure, Admiral Charles Lockwood came aboard, his sea bag over his shoulder. The admiral, a sub skipper back in World War I, was very much respected by most submariners. Many officers referred to him as "Uncle Charlie." He had a habit of personally greeting every returning boat as it tied up at the pier. He liked to go aboard, climb to the bridge, and personally congratulate the skipper, even if the run had been less than stellar. He had been systematically replacing as he could those sub captains who he felt were not being aggressive enough, not willing to press the attack against the enemy. Knowing how debilitating a submarine war patrol could be, he made sure that returning crews were met with medal-award ceremonies, a band, and big vats of ice cream. Lockwood also requisitioned the entire Royal Hawaiian Hotel on the beach at Waikiki as a special resting place for the submariners, officers and sailors alike, when they returned from patrol.

The admiral had also taken the side of his skippers over a bad situation with the torpedoes they were being asked to use. There were far too many duds, and for a time, most of the fish ran much deeper through the water than they were set to do, harmlessly swimming beneath their intended targets. The Navy brass denied there were problems, maintaining that the captains were simply not using the torpedoes correctly. Lockwood stood his ground, proving his point with some specific demonstrations of just how bad—and deadly—the issues were.

The torpedoes were finally fixed. And the attack results improved dramatically.

The admiral traveling as a passenger on his boats further endeared him to submariners. Lockwood could have more easily and quickly flown to where he needed to be, but he preferred to get a firsthand look at what was going on with the boats. The fact that his predecessor died in a plane crash while stateside, causing Lockwood to be promoted to commander of submarines in the Pacific, may have had something to do with his choice of transportation, too.

Now Lockwood's presence gave Gene Fluckey several days' chance to lobby for his own command. And he did just that at every opportunity. He and the admiral also had lengthy conversations about Fluckey's opinions on how the boats might be better utilized. On most points, the men agreed. Where they did not, Fluckey tried to sell his ideas.

Fluckey also had an opportunity to show his familiarity with the submarine when a pesky leak threatened to cause even more serious problems. Should the malfunctioning part fail completely while they were on the surface, they would be unable to dive. That could be fatal if under attack. Or if the leak worsened while they were submerged, they could be in fatal difficulty.

Fluckey told Waterman exactly which hard-to-get-to fitting he believed was causing the leak and how to fix it. That required sending a man—executive officer Robert McNitt, who was tall and skinny enough for the job—into the induction tube, entering from the engine room and crawling a considerable distance up to the malfunctioning fitting. The repair would have to be done while they were submerged.

Indeed, McNitt was able to reach it and get it squared away. They could once again dive and surface the problem boat as necessary. And they would not have to take time during the stopover at Midway for repairs.

After dropping off their passenger and completing some other minor fixes, *Barb* left Midway the next day, March 7, bound for the waters around the Japanese-held territories of Formosa and the Mariana Islands. They soon encountered rough seas. There were waves as high as seventy feet in a seventy-knot gale. They had a rough ride for the next week, and every man aboard, including PCO Gene Fluckey, wondered if they would be able to track and fire at even a single target before they ran out of diesel fuel. Even when the weather improved on March 15, they still saw nothing worth shooting at. They eased farther south, toward Guam and Saipan. Those islands, along with the rest of the Marianas, would still be under Japanese control for another four months. There had been reports of considerable enemy traffic in the area, so Waterman and Fluckey hoped to finally find something on which they could draw a bead.

But it took them more than a week before they got word of a potential major set of targets coming their way.

MARCH 24, 1944

0830: *Changed course to 115 degrees and went to four engine speed in an attempt to intercept reported convoy.*

1400: *Sighted Mavis* patrol plane heading in, distance 7 miles. Submerged to 140 feet in glassy sea.*

1409: *Received two bombs which broke a light bulb. Went to 175 feet.*

1520: *Starting up for a look.*

1524: *Another bomb, not close. Probably just to let us know he is still there.*

1640: *Periscope depth, nothing in sight.*

A message informed *Barb* that a sizable convoy would soon pass through their new patrol area. The submarine would have to run at top speed on the surface most of the day in order to intercept the ships. Just as they drew tantalizingly close to where their potential targets were supposed to steam past, a Japanese patrol plane appeared, spotted them, and zoomed in. Waterman ordered his crew to submerge to 140 feet just as the

---

* A "Mavis" was an Imperial Japanese Navy flying boat used during World War II for maritime patrol duties. They typically carried either two torpedoes or roughly a ton of bombs.

plane dropped two bombs near enough to rattle the diving *Barb*. There was little damage—just a broken light bulb—but the captain took them down another thirty-five feet.

And there they stayed for more than an hour while the convoy they were stalking likely steamed on by, never to be caught and attacked—at least by *Barb*.

That was more than Gene Fluckey could quietly and passively tolerate, even if convention dictated that he should. He and Waterman had a heated discussion in the wardroom. Both men hoped the crew could not hear them. Fluckey was convinced the captain was being far too cautious, that staying submerged for longer than a quarter hour when spotted by aircraft was rarely necessary. Waterman, based on his own training, disagreed. Popping up too soon could easily lead to a bomb on the foredeck and the loss of *Barb* and all aboard.

Though supremely disappointed, Fluckey allowed Waterman to make the call with no further input. It was his boat, after all. In total, they remained submerged for more than two and a half hours, waiting for the lone patrolling aircraft to leave. That dashed any chance for chasing down the convoy and its array of targets.

Neither officer allowed the crew to witness their disagreement. Only a few overheard, but of course every man on board the submarine soon knew all about it. That required that they take sides. Some sided with their skipper, whom they trusted to make the best decision for the good of the boat. Some with the inexperienced Fluckey, because he was duty bound to sink as many enemy ships as he could and bring this damn war to a speedy close. That was just the way he was wired.

Much later in the patrol, Fluckey did tell two of the ship's officers, "If I ever get command and stay down more than fifteen minutes for a Japanese airplane, you have permission to kick me in the rear end."

With the convoy long gone, *Barb* turned to another potential target, one that would not go anywhere. Captain Waterman wanted to reconnoiter a small but important dot of land, Rasa Island, off the coast of Okinawa. The Japanese were reported to have a huge phosphate mining operation there. Phosphates are a key ingredient in explosives. There was hope the submarine could launch a shore barrage on the facilities. Or maybe catch an ore ship there and sink it, hopefully in the harbor, inhibiting traffic in and out.

They saw the mining complex, all right. It was even larger than intelligence data had indicated. But something odd caught their attention. There was a ship in the harbor behaving very erratically, steaming in tight circles, going around and around the island, stopping and starting, speeding up and slowing down, all for no apparent reason.

Both John Waterman and Gene Fluckey felt the vessel was a Q-ship, a warship disguised as a freighter or tanker, but heavily armed. When it attracted an attack, such a ship would suddenly draw back tarps or other coverings and then, decks bristling with guns, counterattack. Q-ships typically had very shallow drafts, too, so torpedoes launched their way simply ran benignly beneath them.

True to form, the captain and the PCO had differing opinions on what to do about this suspected warship. Waterman decided a Q-ship was too big a risk and they would not attack the phosphate facility if the vessel was dashing and darting around the harbor. Fluckey was ready to go after the sneaky vessel while they had the chance to not only take down the bastard but to also clear the way for a gun attack on the facilities.

Fluckey won this one. They would attack as soon as it was dark.

However, before they did, Waterman wanted to creep in close enough that they could take some daylight photos through the periscope of the massive operation on Rasa. But the problem boat was about to suffer yet another couple of issues.

As they were taking pictures, the submarine suddenly and unexpectedly broached, popping to the surface. *Barb* was immediately in clear view of anyone who might be looking their way. An emergency dive got them back down, into hiding. There was no indication anyone had spotted them.

The photos? It turned out they had a bad roll of film and there was nothing at all on the developed footage.

Twenty minutes before midnight on March 28, *Barb* sent three torpedoes—set to run just beneath the surface—hurtling toward the suspected Q-ship. Two of them hit home with huge blasts, the second one cutting the vessel in half. Based on the size of the explosions, the target was confirmed as a Q-ship.

Barb would return to Rasa Island two weeks later. Accompanied by sister boat USS *Steelhead* (SS-280), they launched the kind of aggressive and deadly attack Gene Fluckey so deeply coveted. It was a barrage, using the guns on the deck of the boat, with the intention of damaging or destroying the phosphate facility on the island. At one point during the bombardment, a shell—still holding a live round—jammed up the four-inch gun.

Should it be ejected, hit the deck, and explode, it could severely damage *Barb*, maybe even sink her. Captain Waterman ordered that the attack end and that they withdraw. They would clear the gun later, working carefully and at a safe distance from a possible counterattack from the island.

Fluckey would have none of it. He told the captain he would personally go down onto the deck and clear the casing, and the assault could continue. That meant he would have to have the gun crew captain eject the shell so Fluckey could grab it before it hit the deck and possibly blow up. That was exactly what he did, catching the shell in midair and then casually walking over and tossing it harmlessly over the side into the sea. He dusted off his hands as if he had just taken out the garbage for Marjorie. Then he gave Waterman an exaggerated thumbs-up.

The barrage continued until they were confident the phosphate plant would be out of commission for months to come. There is no way to tally how many Allied soldiers' and sailors' lives they saved.

There had been another incident between the two visits to Rasa in which John Waterman had, without considering other options, gone deep immediately and hidden for more than three hours from aircraft. Fluckey had managed to remain silent then, since no targets were escaping at the time.

In all, Gene Fluckey was pleased with what *Barb* accomplished during the patrol. So were Waterman and the crew. So were the commanders back at Pearl Harbor. Though plagued by bad weather, high seas, and vexing issues with their radar being jammed, everyone was happy they had still managed to strike a powerful if not glamorous blow against the enemy.

Now, low on fuel and groceries, *Barb* pointed the bow back toward Midway. Everyone was in high spirits. That included the submarine's current skipper as well as the man everyone assumed would be her next one. Once back to Midway, Fluckey fully expected to get the keys to USS *Barb*, just as Waterman had promised. Then, after a week or so, he would turn right around and take the submarine back to the war. Waterman had already composed his letter of recommendation that Fluckey be his relief. He even gave Gene the opportunity to read and edit it. Waterman had received word that his orders to report for shore duty as commanding officer of a submarine division were waiting for him at Midway.

Waterman would go on to serve in various staff positions, including commanding submarine squadrons and divisions. After the war, he was back in familiar territory as the CO of the submarine base at Balboa, Canal Zone, in Panama. He was clearly a good commander who ran his submarine the way he was told. Despite *Barb*'s lack of success under his command, he went on to other assignments in which he helped defeat the enemy in World War II and make the Navy stronger afterward.

However, his biggest contribution to the war effort may have come when he knocked on Gene Fluckey's door that night at Pearl Harbor.

When *Barb* docked at Midway at the end of her seventh patrol, with Fluckey ready to relieve Waterman, both officers were shocked to learn that nobody who mattered—including the commanders who actually assigned captains to the various boats in the submarine fleet—knew anything about the swap. Nothing about Fluckey becoming *Barb*'s next skipper. None of them were even aware that Fluckey had been aboard the submarine as a PCO for the boat's seventh run.

To make matters even more complicated, they had already drawn up and delivered orders for someone else to be Waterman's relief. Lieutenant Commander Jake Fyfe—an officer who was well qualified though a full year junior to Fluckey—was twiddling his thumbs at Midway, waiting to take over for Waterman as the CO of *Barb*.

The done deal had somehow come undone.

It was a familiar feeling for the ambitious young submarine officer. There was the similar ordeal when he left the *S-42* behind in Panama, transferring to New London for what he had been led to believe would be the start of his first submarine command. This one hurt far more, though. As far as he knew, all he had to do was return from the patrol with the boat afloat and *Barb* was his. Then he could take her back out and win the war.

Now, though, it appeared that there was no way the decisions of the division commanders could be overridden. All the pieces were in place and Gene Fluckey did not have a position on the board.

Then a thought occurred to him. There was one very important person who was fully aware that he had ridden *Barb* as a PCO. A person who knew the magnitude of the plans Fluckey had formulated for how he would fight the boat once she was under his command.

Of course, this might be too minor a situation to even get it on the man's desk, and the man might ultimately decide it was not worth his time and effort to straighten out this mess.

Gene Fluckey decided it was worth a shot anyway.

CHAPTER NINE

SILHOUETTED BY THE MOON

26 JUNE 1945

Surface patrolling south along SAKHALIN.

1655: CONTACT #3: Through a remarkable atmospheric lens sighted a Convoy at a range later determined to be 40-45,000 yards. With this lens effect, the Convoy appeared to be viewed from about a 5 degree elevation, all ships being on this side of the horizon in miniature with bow waves visible and no parts of the ships sticking up above our normal horizon. Thermal waves were apparent throughout this sector. Commenced end around.

Commander Eugene Fluckey had seen such an odd atmospheric phenomenon before, but never so pronounced as this one, nor anything nearly so helpful to what he wanted to accomplish on *Barb*'s twelfth war patrol.

From the bridge of the submarine, and thanks to an impressive event similar to a mirage, Fluckey and his lookouts were able to clearly see a Japanese convoy as much as twenty-five miles away. Normally, from the bridge or lookout platforms in the shears of a *Gato*-class boat, or even when using the magnification of the periscope fully extended to its maximum height while on the surface, they could only see about nine or ten miles to the horizon. Smoke from the stacks of larger ships might give them a clue there was a convoy out there, but even that would typically be from no more than ten miles or so.

After the rocket attack on Shari, their only real action had been the trawler where they picked up the POW. Then they had come dangerously close to running their beautiful submarine onto the beach in Patience Bay while chasing smokestacks. Since then, with the diversion tactics successfully completed and the freedom to search out and attack wherever and whatever they wanted, the run had turned cold and monotonous.

Now here was a nice convoy to stalk. With the advance view offered by the atmospheric lens, they should have ample opportunity to get into the best position to send every vessel to the bottom of the Sea of Okhotsk. Fluckey sent *Barb* running on the surface to do what submariners called an end-around, taking an angle and speed to get ahead of the likely course of the targets and set up to shoot.

As they sped in that direction, the mirage continued, like an image on a movie screen. They could even see aircraft flying above the convoy. That further confirmed a worthy quarry. Fluckey invited crewmembers not on watch to come up onto the deck and see the odd vision on the horizon. Others took a peek through the periscope.

The sun was still bright when they arrived at the spot in the sea where they would wait for their targets to steam past.

1910: *Ahead of Convoy. In view of no darkness tonight—*
late sunset, long twilight, full moon and after
previous days of fog, a sparkling clear, cold day—
decided on a submerged attack now.

1920: *Submerged. Range unknown. However, enemy may*
have us spotted as easily as we have him. Closing
at high speed . . . Looks like the Japs are
determined to get these through.

Forty minutes later, the first masts of the ships in the convoy appeared at the horizon as Fluckey and his XO, James Webster, took turns watching for them. The captain called out, "Battle stations, torpedoes!" and the atmosphere in the submarine instantly went electric as the distinctive battle stations alarm sounded.

Fluckey made a quick check with the torpedo rooms to confirm what they had loaded in the tubes. Reloading in the midst of a shooting battle was often problematic. *Barb* had six tubes at the bow and four at the stern. She had left Pearl Harbor with all the torpedoes she could carry, twenty-four fish, sixteen up front and eight aft. There was no way, of course, to move torpedoes from one end of the boat to the other while at sea. Because all attacks so far on this run had used the deck guns and rockets, the boat still had its full complement of torpedoes. This convoy might just be worth using most of them.

All but two of the loaded torpedoes were the usual weapons, Mark 18s, the most effective submarine weapon in the war. Fully sixty-five percent of the torpedoes fired by subs in 1945 would be the Mark 18. By the end of the war, more than a million tons of Japanese shipping would be sunk by that particular model. But *Barb* also had two new experimental acoustically homing torpedoes, the Mark 28, loaded and ready, one forward, one aft. Fluckey was anxious to try them out but he told everyone to save the sophisticated new fish for any destroyers or other escorts that would be coming their way after the sub had announced its presence in a very obvious manner.

Primed, ready to go, hearts racing, the periscope beautifully filled with the approaching enemy convoy, everyone on the sub was again ready to recapture some of the spectacular success they had enjoyed on patrol number eleven.

But then, with the ST radar showing the ships drawing closer, about to be caught in *Barb*'s web:

2028: *ST range 11,000 yards. Angle on the bow zero.*

2037: *Convoy turned towards beach sharply, giving large port angle on the bow. Commenced approach on far seaward escort, a TERUTSUKI, since we have now been cut off by base course change.*

The convoy had dodged to the west, making a very sharp turn away from where *Barb* lay in ambush. The targets were moving much closer to the shore. Fluckey deduced that now that the Japanese ships had left Russian territorial waters, they had decided to seek the relative safety of the shallower seas closer to Sakhalin. The Japanese were trying to make it more difficult for a US submarine to stalk them, should one happen to be out there in the deeper water. Whether the enemy knew it or not, the tactic was working quite well.

The skipper asked one of his officers, Lieutenant Max Duncan, to check the identification manual and try to determine the type of ship that was closest to them. It, at least, was a possible target even if the others were not. Not yet, anyway. As Duncan alternately thumbed through the manual and peered through the 'scope, Fluckey began lining up to take a shot at the only vessel they had any hopes of hitting for now.

"Captain, the destroyer?" Duncan reported. "She's a *Terutsuki*-class. That's the best antisubmarine destroyer they have."

"And she is going to look good standing on her end as she goes down," Fluckey replied with his typical bravado. The assessment of the potential target had not deterred Fluckey at all.

He ordered the door of the tube that housed the Mark 28 "homer" torpedo—one of the new experimental weapons—to be opened and made ready. Then, when they were as close as they dared get—just beyond the range of the wicked destroyer's sonar—he ordered, "Fire four!"

Every man on the submarine could hear and feel the pronounced push as the torpedo was flushed from the tube and, with only a slight pause, started its run directly toward the enemy warship. A quick calculation confirmed that at this range, it would take the homing fish almost two minutes to sniff out the noise of the destroyer's propellor and then blow her out of the water.

But thirty-three seconds into the run, the Mark 28 simply disappeared. No sound whatsoever on *Barb*'s sonar. Everyone in the conning tower waited, well past two minutes. Still nothing. The only thing worse would have been to hear the new homing torpedo turn around and come back toward the sub that launched it, zeroing in on the wrong noise source. That had happened with other less advanced torpedoes—called a circular run—and sometimes with fatal results. That was what had taken down another of the war's most successful submarines and her legendary skipper, USS *Tang* (SS-306) and Richard O'Kane, back in October 1944. The captain and eight other men survived but the sub and seventy-eight crewmembers were lost.

Now, with a deadly, submarine-killing warship only a short distance away, a complete failure like this one was bad enough. Especially if the enemy had heard and could see the spot of the launch of the torpedo on their sonar.

A quick peek through the periscope suggested the target destroyer's crew was unaware of just how close they had come to having a very bad day. They remained on the same southbound course, parallel to the convoy they were faithfully shielding. They still had no idea *Barb* was out there taking shots at them.

Eugene Fluckey was livid, but he kept his composure for the sake of the crew. They were not finished. He promptly ordered them to start making another end-around so they could catch up with the convoy once more, and this time finish the job. These targets were not going to be allowed to get away.

In anticipation of their eventual success, the captain ordered that more beer be placed in the cooler. If any man on board doubted Gene Fluckey's determination, that one command would certainly set him straight.

Later, in a special and very opinionated addition to his report for *Barb*'s twelfth patrol, Fluckey would be specific about his feelings on the subject of submarines and torpedoes. He wrote: "The torpedo has fulfilled its purpose. Its day, in this war, is passing. It is believed that, in the not too distant future, with the anticipated increase in tempo of air strikes, and the lack of air opposition, that lifeguard duties will be taken over, more capably and more efficiently by PT boats. Thus, those of us, not specially equipped for the last good area, must stagnate and slowly slip into oblivion, or look to a new main battery—rockets. The rocket is not a toy. Its possibilities are tremendous . . ."

Fluckey was not totally accurate in his prediction. Modern submarines continue to carry torpedoes, but he was certainly correct when he predicted that rockets would one day become a primary submarine weapon.

Barb raced at flank speed on the surface even though there was a full moon. They were making a lot of noise, and the warmth of their diesel exhaust was shining brilliantly white in the cold air. They simply had to get ahead of the convoy once again. Fluckey had decided by now that the Japanese knew they were out there. There was no reason for the submarine to take precautions and attempt to remain concealed. Truth was, the enemy may have known it all along. That could have been the reason for the convoy's hard right turn toward shallow water in the first place. And even if they did not know there was a US submarine trailing them, they certainly would once ships in the convoy started exploding from torpedo hits all around them.

Barb soon had confirmation of their captain's belief.

> 2234: *One or more escorts, probably that d—TERUTSUKI*
> *gave us several broadsides at 12,000 yards. Gunfire*
> *was seen and heard and pointed in our direction.*
> *No splashes were observed by C.O. or O.O.D. All*
> *others had been cleared from the bridge. We are*
> *brightly silhouetted by moon.*

Barb had once again caught up with the target convoy, which still ran as close to the shoreline as they dared. Fluckey had guided his submarine in to within a little less than seven miles. He hoped to sneak closer and launch a bit of hell toward the enemy ships. But an escort or two—maybe the treacherous *Terutsuki*-class destroyer, though Fluckey could not quite bring himself to use the word "damn" in his eventual report—apparently saw them in the glow of the moon and started shooting. Though *Barb*'s crew could not see where the shells were landing, they could definitely hear their whine as they zoomed close.

The sub turned away and ran at flank speed until the shelling stopped, and then hurried on down the coast to again wait on the convoy, assuming they would anchor for the night in shallow water. There the enemy knew they would be relatively safe from that American submarine wolfpack they likely assumed was after them. Fluckey had deduced that the vessels were probably passing the night in the little harbor near Anaiwa Misaki, just across the narrow strip of land that formed the eastern side of Patience Bay. There was only sixty to eighty feet of water there, not nearly enough for a submarine as big as *Barb* to maneuver, attack, duck, and safely escape. And the escorts that had fired at them would still be protecting the convoy.

Fluckey and his crew were sure that the ships would eventually move southward again and would have to pass right in front of them. All they had to do was get south of the convoy, wait, and knock off as many of them as they could once they were in deeper water. It had become a familiar dance for American submarines by then. The difference was that now the waltz often took place in waters, like the Sea of Okhotsk, where Japanese ships had not been challenged often, if at all.

Sure enough, just before 0800 on June 27, the two-step resumed. One of the lookouts above the bridge reported the convoy was moving again, coming right at them. *Barb* submerged and moved in closer to land, near enough to be able to take their pick of targets but still in deep enough water beneath their keel to get below potential shells and depth charges.

> 0749: *Contact with Convoy coming down coast deep inside ten fathom* curve. Dived and commenced closing coast. Ocean an oily calm.*
>
> 0810: *Surface haze lifted near coast. Visibility excellent.*

---

* A fathom is six feet of water. The "ten-fathom curve" would be a point at which the water would be about sixty feet deep, barely enough for a submarine the size of *Barb* to operate while submerged.

Finally, *Barb* was in prime position to finish what they had started. However, there was no way for Fluckey and his brave crew to anticipate just how long the whole thing would eventually take. The skipper had already become known to all as Lucky Fluckey, primarily because of his daring action on the submarine's eleventh patrol, his fourth as CO. That action still had the entire submarine force buzzing. Some in awe. Some out of jealousy for the attention afforded Fluckey's boat.

Attempting to wreak havoc on this elusive enemy convoy, one first revealed to them in an eerie apparition in the sky, would ultimately consume two and a half more days of tense maneuvering. That action would necessitate a tremendous amount of skill, tenacity, and bravery.

And, yes, more than a little bit of serendipity.

CHAPTER TEN

THE WORST SUBMARINE IN THE FLEET

Eugene Fluckey and Admiral Charles Lockwood had many things in common. One of them was that during their careers in the Silent Service, both officers served—at different times—aboard the submarine USS *Bonita*. Lockwood was the boat's commissioning skipper when the *Barracuda*-class V-boat was put into service in May of 1926. The term "V-boat" does not mean they were a class of nearly identical ships, as is typical, but instead refers to this bunch being built as part of the same authorization. These nine V-boats, though manufactured as part of the same program, were actually quite different from one another in many respects.

Bonita was originally designated as *V-3*. She carried that name during her first assignment, patrolling the East Coast of the US, the Caribbean, and then the Pacific Ocean from San Diego to

Hawaii. She got her new name in March of 1931 and, true to her problematic history, it was misspelled. The intent was to name her for the bonito, a finned fish in the same family as the tuna and mackerel. Once all the forms and correspondence were completed and somebody noticed there was no such fish as a "bonita," the decision was made to simply leave it as it was rather than try to straighten out all that Navy paperwork.

"Bonita" means "pretty" in Spanish. This particular vessel was anything but pretty.

After more than a decade of limited service, and none of that in combat, the Navy decided *Bonita* was no longer needed. In February 1937, she was brought back through the Panama Canal and up the East Coast to the Philadelphia Navy Yard. There she was taken out of commission, had most equipment removed, had all hatch covers padlocked shut, and was tied up at a pier to await any possible future service. As far as the official plan stated, she was still in reserve should she ever again be considered necessary.

Few believed the old and clunky boat would sail again. Not with all the problems that she had had during her time in service. But then, with Japan and the ever-present and concerning vulnerability of the Panama Canal, *Bonita* was put back to work, and only three years later. The sub was recommissioned in September of 1940. She made the run from Philadelphia to her new home port, Coco Solo in the Canal Zone, two months later. Many of the newer submarine brass in the US Navy were miffed that money was spent and production capacity wasted to get the old and unwieldy boat back into service. They argued that both of those precious commodities could have been better used for the construction of the new and far more capable boats. There were still many in high places in the Navy who doubted the value of submarines at all. That is, beyond shielding the fleet and guarding shoreline, bays, and harbors. *Bonita* would be just fine—and much more inexpensively deployed—for just such limited duty, they argued. "Instead of a fish out of water, she was a bird in hand," one crewmember wrote.

It was June 11, 1941, when Gene Fluckey, now a lieutenant junior grade but otherwise very disappointed in the lack of advancement in his naval career, officially met up with his new boat, the *Bonita*. That was while she was on maneuvers in the vicinity of Bermuda. Her squadron commander was determined to make the best use of her, despite the boat's limitations. He was keeping her exceptionally busy, constantly at sea, conducting training and continually fixing whatever broke on her, all in an effort to find ways to make her more useful.

But Fluckey was disappointed because he had so recently left Panama and *S-42* with the promise of being given a submarine command of his own in New London. Disappointed because he had to leave Marjorie and Barbara behind in Connecticut when he got sent right back to the Canal Zone. And concerned that, from what he was hearing, it would be unlikely he would be able to move his family back to Panama anytime soon. That was because of the scarcity of housing there for dependents during the war-fear buildup.

On the other hand, Fluckey agreed that the submarine mission around the Canal Zone was important duty. Intelligence had confirmed that the Japanese had developed a new class of big submarine, a boat that easily had range enough to do a round-trip voyage from Japan to Panama and back, and it could do so by making better than twenty-three knots while running on the surface. Even more worrisome, the new IJN boat had a unique capability for submarines. Each sub could carry four airplanes on its decks, housed in covered "hangars." Those aircraft could be launched by catapult while the submarine was on the surface. The planes would be able to fly off and do their damage while the submarine submerged and remained hidden to await their return. Then the aircraft that survived their mission could fly back and be recovered by the I-boat, which would then dive and disappear. It was like a small aircraft carrier that could hide. The consensus was that these new subs and their airplanes were designed and constructed primarily to attack US military facilities—including those on the West Coast—but especially the Panama Canal.

There was considerable U-boat activity in the Caribbean as well. Deadly activity. The German submarines also were capable of extremely long-range operation. Japan and Germany would be active allies should war break out, whether or not the United States joined in. With Hitler's U-boats already torpedoing and sinking US vessels that were believed to be carrying war matériel to Great Britain, President Franklin Roosevelt had instructed US warships to shoot to kill if they spotted a U-boat. Thus it was that *Bonita* was actually on a war footing well before World War II started. But as it happened, she would not shoot at or sink anything.

The United States wanted to do whatever was necessary to avoid engaging in another world war. Not in Europe. Not in the Pacific. Memories were long. Most saw the Great War—the "War to End All Wars"—as a waste of lives, money, and combat equipment, with very little to show for it. Many were convinced that all that suffering and loss occurred as a part of a conflict that was never a direct threat to the United States. They did not want to have to make such a decision again. That was one reason the US had insisted on such a harsh set of conditions for the surrender of Germany—reparations that led to the rise of fierce nationalism and the Nazi Party in that country, and the ascent of a leader named Adolf Hitler.

Everyone from aviation hero Charles Lindbergh to renowned author Ernest Hemingway to the president of the United States lobbied to remain on the sidelines. President Franklin Roosevelt had resisted the pleas to join the conflict even though they came from solid allies on that continent. And even if Great Britain and other friends in Europe were suffering greatly from Hitler's aggression, there was little sentiment for once again entering into a war there. And a two-front war would be the worst possible outcome, most in the Roosevelt administration believed. Unwinnable. So diplomacy continued to avoid war with Japan. And Roosevelt did what he could to help but refused to go to war on behalf of the European nations that were being brutally pounded and boldly invaded by the Nazis.

Meanwhile, the US military watched developments while continuing to prepare as best they could should war come. Leaders openly claimed that if the country was dragged into another foreign war, it would not come as a surprise to anyone. The fighting forces would be ready.

One key preparation by the Navy was the design considerations on the new *Gato*- and *Balao*-class submarines.

Modifications such as the greatly improved air-conditioning systems on those boats. That was not necessarily for crew comfort but to minimize condensation, which could be damaging to the complex electrical systems on the new subs. This was a factor because many in the Navy believed there would be war with the Empire of Japan and it would be fought in the hot, humid South Pacific and Southeast Asia.

Also, the new boats would have a much longer operating range and a greater choice of deck guns than previous submersibles. That was because they would likely have to crisscross the huge Pacific and would necessarily be required to travel and deliver much of their punch while on the surface.

Better radar and communications systems were being finalized. Newer and more sophisticated torpedoes were undergoing development and testing as well: weapons that packed a more powerful punch, that could be set to run truer to their intended course with less visible wake, and even a torpedo that could acoustically home in on the screws of a target ship and be more likely to strike its objective.

That preparation for a looming war was what sent Eugene Fluckey back to Panama, but his frustration intensified when he joined *Bonita* in Bermuda and rode his new ship back to the base at Coco Solo. There was nothing new or cutting-edge about this old boat.

The commanding officer of the squadron that included the *Bonita*, Captain Ralph Christie—the one who had been putting his V-boats and their crews through their paces to try to squeeze out just a bit more capability—had found some of the older subs to be useful. But not the *Bonita*. Christie had already pronounced to anyone who would listen that this one was the worst of all the V-boats, and quite possibly the worst vessel in the US Navy's submarine fleet.

And he had good reasons for his low opinion. The boat's diesel engines were grossly underpowered. They never were able to deliver the design speed of twenty-one knots while on the surface. Even worse, her fuel tanks leaked badly, which left an oil slick on the surface when submerged, a big problem for a vessel that depended on stealth. And nobody had been able to stop the seepage so far, not in the decade and a half she had been in service or the many times she had been in port for a refit.

Fluckey was appalled to learn that the submarine, as designed, required almost two minutes to fully submerge once the command to dive was issued. Should a shooting war happen, such a slow dive would never do. If the sub was on the surface, once an enemy airplane was spotted, the goal for most submariners was to get their boat down in less than one minute. Anything longer would allow the attacking plane more than enough time to bomb and strafe.

Then, when *Bonita* actually made that first dive with Fluckey aboard, the young lieutenant was shocked to learn that his new vessel was not even capable of that two-minute dive. Not even close. If the dive angle was anything greater than two degrees— that is the down-angle on the bow in relation to the horizontal, which in most boats was typically about ten degrees—then she might abruptly veer toward the bottom of the sea, completely out of control. That meant the quickest the boat could get under was, in reality, closer to six minutes. Six minutes!

After that first dive on the *Bonita*, a frustrated Fluckey told his new captain that should war come, the boat would not last through her first encounter with the enemy. In fact, Fluckey predicted, she would likely be sunk by a pilot who was still in the ready room at his air base when *Bonita* began making the dive. And Fluckey was not joking by much.

That was, he decided, a good opportunity to apply his motto of "no problems, just solutions." Utilizing his engineering skills and sharp, analytical mind, Fluckey devised a new way to dive the old boat that no one had ever considered. This maneuver allowed for a rather sharp twenty-degree down angle. But to keep her from becoming unstable, he would offset the force that tended to make the vessel erratic by simultaneously pumping water into ballast tanks. Testing the process was dangerous, but Fluckey convinced the captain it was not nearly as dangerous as a Japanese or German plane putting a bomb down the bridge hatch into the conning tower.

His idea worked. *Bonita* was ultimately able to get beneath the surface and find relative safety in just under one minute. Learning to accomplish the maneuver led to some anxious moments for the officers and sailors aboard, but they were pleased when they saw that Fluckey's idea had succeeded, and that it could help save the submarine if an enemy plane were ever up there, circling, angling for an attack. The maneuver was soon adopted by other older boats in the fleet.

It was hard not to like the redheaded, freckle-faced—and often sunburned—young officer, but Fluckey did manage to ruffle the feathers of many of his shipmates and squadron brass. He pushed for change and wanted to find new and better ways to do things. He had officers and crew constantly drilling, practicing different tactics anytime they had the boat at sea. Captain Christie had decided that some of the boat's original crew, men who were plank owners—those who were on the boat when she was commissioned—were the only ones who could make the old girl behave. That was true to a point, but it also meant that several of the men were over sixty years old, and some did not appreciate the eagerness of their newest officer, especially the chief petty officers. Fluckey would later claim that he had to retire one chief when the man turned sixty-five.

Additionally, not everyone serving on *Bonita* was yet convinced that war was inevitable. Some preferred to simply enjoy the tropical climate and the other benefits of being stationed in a reasonably entertaining place and not devote so much time and effort to drills, experiments, or maintenance on the sub.

Duty in Panama in 1940 and 1941 could be quite boring. *Bonita*'s job was to range westward from the canal, looking for Japanese submarines, especially the big ones with the aircraft riding piggyback on their decks. In the unlikely event that Japan was crazy enough to launch a surprise attack on the United States, the canal might be a prime target. Damaging the ship passageway through the isthmus would mean that traffic bound from one great ocean to the other—warships, cargo ships, troop ships, most of which were specifically designed so they could fit through the locks and waterways in Panama—would have to go instead around the stormy southern tip of South America. That would add weeks to the transit.

Fluckey, always ready to learn, took advantage of the opportunity to study the tactics and leadership style of the skipper and his more experienced submarine officers. He was already deciding how he would run his own boat, in peacetime or war-time, once he had the helm. In many instances, he knew he would do things quite a bit differently from what he was observing. No reflection on the COs—they were merely doing it the way they had been taught.

Then, especially good news: Fluckey was finally able to secure housing for his family. His wife and daughter would be able to rejoin him in Panama, it appeared, before Christmas. They should be there and settled in time to spend some wonderful holidays together. Barbara Ann was now three and a half, old enough that Christmas was especially exciting for her, and now it appeared Gene could make sure Santa located the little girl way down there in the Canal Zone.

The plan was for his wife and daughter to travel by Navy transport ship from Connecticut to Panama with needed household possessions in stowage belowdecks. However, the means of transportation had Marjorie a bit worried: despite the government's best efforts to avoid panic, some Americans were still learning about the toll the German U-boats were taking on ships in the Atlantic off the East Coast of the US. Mrs. Fluckey certainly had bad memories about having been torpedoed while at sea, even though she had been very young at the time.

Gene assured her in his letters home that she had nothing to worry about. He convinced her that the Navy would never put dependents on a ship if they did not believe it to be reasonably safe. There would be escort ships, too, to deflect any German attention. And if things did appear to be too dangerous, he was sure the voyage would be canceled. Marjorie stayed busy enough, packing, selecting which Christmas ornaments she would bring with her, putting other possessions into storage, and otherwise getting ready for the trip. That left less time for fretting. Besides, if that was what it took for them to spend the holidays together, she was willing to climb aboard that Navy transport with Barbara Ann and head southward. They had not seen each other since June.

Then came the disappointing news that their departure date on the transport would be delayed until December 31. There would be no Christmas or New Year's Day with her husband.

But to the rescue came Gene's brother, Jim. (Jim had, by the way, changed his last name years before from Fluckey to Snowden, their mother's maiden name. That was to avoid the hazing such a moniker could cause in school or on the playground. Their other brother, Ken, had changed his last name to Flocke. Gene never even considered doing such a thing.) Thankfully, Jim had found a way to get his niece and sister-in-law down to Panama for the reunion and have them there before Christmas. He had finagled a booking on a luxury liner, and they were scheduled to depart on December 14. Marjorie's letter, letting Gene know that they would be there in time for the holidays after all, was dropped into the mail to him on December 6.

Then, on December 7, 1941, the world tilted on its axis.

Fluckey and the crew of *Bonita* received a secret message early on the evening of December 7, confirming what they had been hearing already. A state of war existed between the United States and Japan. They were to begin preparations immediately for their first war patrol, which would take them from Coco Solo, through the canal to Balboa on the Pacific side of Panama, and then into the suddenly more dangerous Pacific. The transit through the canal on December 10 took seven hours. Then another hour negotiating the protective minefield that had been laid at the entrance, just in case war ever came.

Instead of Christmas with his wife and daughter, Fluckey spent Christmas 1941 crisscrossing the primary Pacific shipping lanes leading to and from the canal. For three weeks, they steamed westward each day from sunrise to high noon, then turned 180 degrees from that course and steamed to the east until sunset. Ever conscious of saving precious diesel fuel, they spent the hours of darkness sitting perfectly still, quiet and unlit, on the surface, batteries always fully charged, ready to dive if any ship or plane approached.

Bonita was looking for anything Japanese—airplane, ship, or submarine. They saw nothing but US Navy vessels and the occasional freighter or tanker. Their toughest job was keeping from getting run over or bombed by one of their sister warships or planes, which was made more difficult by continuing issues with the submarine. They did not flood the torpedo tubes even once, not even to test their capabilities.

There was no action, no casualties on the run. Two crewmen did become ill, one of them with what was diagnosed as a mild case of German measles, but both recovered quickly and were back on duty for the return run to Coco Solo.

The entire report for USS *Bonita*'s first official patrol of World War II required less than two typed pages.

The submarine returned to Panama on New Year's Day, 1942. An anxious Fluckey learned that there was no longer any non-military transportation moving between the US and Panama. That included cruise ships. Those dependents who were already in the Canal Zone were being evacuated to the States. That was no surprise. The day President Roosevelt and Congress officially declared war on Japan—December 8—Germany had announced a declaration of war against the United States as part of Hitler's treaty with the Empire. When the first Japanese bomb fell in Hawaii, America was in the middle of the dreaded two-front war they had vowed to avoid.

Bonita anchored off the naval base, awaiting permission to dock and go ashore. Gene Fluckey was frantic. Had Marjorie and Barbara Ann made it onto the ocean liner and had it completed its itinerary all the way to Panama before travel was halted? Or had the trip been canceled before they departed? Was it possible that they were in Panama now, in that new housing he had so happily arranged for them, *waiting* for him to get back from his first war patrol? Or had they been put right back on a ship and sent home, to their recently vacated cottage in New London, Connecticut? Or were they somewhere in between, put into a strange port when all transportation stopped moving?

When he finally got back to his quarters, Fluckey worked his way through the stack of letters from Marjorie. That was when he learned that their ocean liner trip had indeed been canceled before it departed. The news was at first a great relief. At least for now, his girls were safe there in New London, far safer than they would be in the Canal Zone, in the vicinity of a prime target for not only the Japanese ships and planes but also for the German U-boats.

Then the disappointment settled in. As discouraged as he was, Gene wrote long letters to Marjorie, telling her all he was allowed to say, to keep her spirits up. He did not mention much else about his duty, about his being on the worst boat in the fleet. Not about the strong possibility that the next enemy air assault might well be on the Panama Canal. Nothing concerning the considerable danger of steaming on *Bonita* out into the Pacific to meet submarines and other warships that were far more capable and dangerous than his vessel would ever be.

Instead, he kept everything upbeat, always accentuating the positive. One of his letters ended with a strong, encouraging prediction.

"The war will be over by Barbara Ann's birthday," he promised.

That would be March 19, 1942. A mere three months after it all started.

Fluckey felt much better, just writing down that hopeful, happy date.

But he also knew in his heart of hearts that it was impossibly optimistic.

CHAPTER ELEVEN

GETTING *BARB*

25 APR. (1944)

    0530   Crossed International date line and repeated
            this day.

25 APR.

    1705   Moored Midway.

The official name of Midway Island is Midway Atoll. It barely qualifies as an island, being only about two and a half square miles in area. It lies about halfway between Hawaii and Japan, which explains the name. Technically it is part of the Hawaiian archipelago but is not a part of the state of Hawaii. Early in the atoll's history, its primary economic value was for its bird droppings, or guano, which is used as a fertilizer. Later it became a coaling station for ships, then a fuel stop for Pan American Airlines' "flying boats" and other aircraft. There was even a Pan American Hotel there for the passengers during overnight layovers, as well as for military personnel and other visitors.

Midway's importance skyrocketed in 1940 as tensions increased between the US and Japan. Naval Air Station Midway was completed that year. Many considered the speck of land to be second in importance only to Pearl Harbor should it ever become necessary to defend the West Coast of the United States from the Empire of Japan. Two Japanese destroyers attacked Midway on December 7, 1941, but they were driven away by American planes in what some consider the first military victory by the US in World War II. But six months later, in June of 1942, Midway was once again attacked by the Japanese, with the intent of seizing the strategic atoll. However, the IJN had a second goal: to lure the US Navy's aircraft carriers into a virtual ambush and finish the job of destroying the fleet, the task begun back in December. The Battle of Midway went the other way, though, and would prove to be a major victory for the US and a loss to the Empire's navy from which they would never recover.

A month after that crucial battle, a submarine tender was permanently stationed at Midway. Later, a floating dock was constructed to host submarines. The island quickly became a key staging, repair, replenishment, and refueling area for the subs that were so busily creating havoc with Japanese shipping, military or not. The atoll was perfectly located to top off fuel tanks and do most repairs. It became a regular stopover for submarines coming from or returning to Hawaii from the Central and South Pacific and all the way to the Sea of Japan and the Yellow Sea. That greatly extended their operating range and time on patrol. Soon, unless designated for a longer turnaround or more extensive refit, the subs would be sent back out on patrol from Midway without returning to Hawaii or other ports in Australia. At its peak, more than five thousand military personnel were stationed on Midway, many of them serving the submarine base there. The former Pan Am layover had become a key installation for the Navy, especially for the Silent Service. It would also be a key stop for Lieutenant Commander Eugene Fluckey and his hopes for submarine command.

Midway was the destination for USS *Barb* as she returned from her seventh war patrol, her second in the Pacific under John R. Waterman. The run ended up being a total of fifty-five days, a long time for submarine patrols at that time. Captain Waterman made note in his report that the men seemed fatigued as they docked at Midway on April 25. They may have been tired, but they were also proud to have sunk the Q-ship and bombarded the phosphate plant on Rasa Island. Everyone aboard was in reasonably good spirits.

The crew also knew change was coming. Their next skipper, assumedly, had already been on board for this patrol. Most of the men liked him. He had already made promises that *Barb*'s eighth run would be spectacular. Maybe even fun. For starters, a new ice cream freezer was installed before leaving Pearl Harbor for the just-completed patrol. It was so popular that Eugene Fluckey told the men he would double the amount of mix they took with them on the eighth patrol. Ice cream would be as readily available as coffee.

As expected, Waterman had orders waiting at Midway for his new position as a submarine squadron commander. Only a change-of-command ceremony on *Barb* awaited. Then Waterman would be off to Hawaii. But before that came word that none of the people in charge of the base knew anything about

Fluckey having ridden along on *Barb* as her PCO. Nothing about any deal for Fluckey to relieve Waterman. Indeed, Lieutenant Commander Jake Fyfe had already received orders to take the sub out on her eighth war patrol. Fyfe was waiting for the change-of-command ceremony so he could take charge of preparations.

Solutions, not problems. Fluckey went to work trying to fix this mess.

First of all, he knew he had an ace in the hole: an eyewitness who could confirm that he had ridden *Barb* as her prospective commander. That ace was the big boss, Admiral Charles Lockwood, who had hitched the ride on *Barb* from Pearl Harbor to Midway almost two months before. Uncle Charlie had also witnessed some of Fluckey's innovative leadership. The two officers had had many discussions about how the boats could be made more productive. If anybody could straighten out this snafu, Uncle Charlie could. That is, if he would even consider the situation before Jake Fyfe and *Barb* steamed back toward Japan. While Lockwood often got involved with the assignments of specific skippers for his boats, he was not necessarily quick to override the staff responsible for that chore.

Fluckey did a quick sales pitch to the squadron commander on Midway. It worked. The commander agreed to radio a message to Lockwood and see if he was willing to weigh in.

In less than a day, Lockwood approved Fluckey as CO for *Barb* and made certain Fyfe would get the next relief assignment. As it happened, that quick change worked out well for both COs, for the submarine service, and for the war effort.

Jake Fyfe assumed command of USS *Batfish* (SS-310) a few

weeks later, in mid-May 1944, and took her out on her third war patrol. Over the next four runs, Fyfe and *Batfish* would claim thirteen ships sunk. They also completed one of the most remarkable accomplishments of the war: In February 1945, on *Batfish*'s sixth patrol, Fyfe and his crew sank three Japanese submarines in a little over three days—submarines that were reportedly loaded with top Japanese officers fleeing the Philippines, accompanied by their mistresses, and hauling a fortune in gold. Fyfe would be awarded the Navy Cross for that feat.

On April 28, Eugene Fluckey officially became a submarine skipper, and he was about to show the world that he was among the best to ever hold that job. To make certain there would be no more last-minute issues or reversals, John Waterman rushed up the change-of-command ceremony before anything else happened. That was a mere two days after Lockwood's quick approval.

Fluckey got busy with a training schedule he had already made up for his crew. He wanted to make certain everybody knew how the new "Old Man"—while skippers of naval vessels were often referred to as the Old Man, Gene Fluckey was thirty years old when he became a CO—would be running *Barb* from now on. In front of the crew mustered on the deck, he pointedly tossed overboard the previous captain's list of infractions and punishments for various minor violations by crewmembers. Fluckey assured them there would be no captain's mast on his boat, none of the hearings in which accused sailors had to answer for their sins and learn what their punishment would be. On *Barb,* men were expected to do what they were supposed to do, to play when they were supposed to play but work when they needed to work. Their new skipper trusted them to do just that. That, he told them, included always pressing the attack and sinking enemy ships. In the few days remaining before they were back at sea, he intended to show them more changes he would initiate.

Barb was scheduled to depart on patrol on May 21. The way seemed clear for Fluckey to take his boat and crew and do some serious damage.

But then, out of the blue, he received a very concerning message from Uncle Charlie. The admiral was coming out to Midway and wanted to sit down and have a talk with Fluckey. That chat would occur on May 20, one day before *Barb* was to leave tropical Midway Atoll for the cold waters north of Hokkaido.

Surely Fluckey was not about to have the rug pulled from beneath him again! Was his aggressive move to have Lockwood intervene in the CO mess coming back to bite him? All he knew to do was not worry about the audience with Lockwood and go ahead getting ready for *Barb*'s eighth run. At least until he knew something different.

Those preparations included sea trials and, as they often did, undergoing a much-too-real indoctrination, which was having a couple of depth charges dropped from an aircraft and detonated near the submarine. This was for the benefit of any crewmembers who had never experienced such an unnerving event. It was also a test for *Barb* since such nearby explosions might reveal undiscovered leaks or create new ones. All went well this time, although a number of lights—and the nerves of some new crewmen—inside the boat were shattered by the "friendly" depth charges.

The crew and support personnel were just completing loading when Admiral Lockwood arrived and crossed over the brow onto the boat. Uncle Charlie had a serious look on his face. His first question for Fluckey as he came aboard the submarine—just after "Good morning, Gene"—was "How do you feel about taking *Barb* out on this patrol?"

"We're ready in all respects, sir," Fluckey shot back with no hesitation. And he meant it. Then he looked the admiral in the eye and asked, "How many ships do you want us to sink?"

Lockwood may have brought a serious face aboard, but now it changed to a slightly bemused expression.

"How many do you think you can sink, Gene?"

Without blinking, Fluckey promised five kills, then asked his boss what type of enemy vessels he preferred they send to the bottom. Freighters, tankers, warships? Lockwood assured his newest skipper that five Japanese vessels of any type would be fine with him. In truth, the most successful submarine patrol of the war so far had sunk five ships.

Lockwood then informed Fluckey that *Barb* would, as ordered, be operating in the Sea of Okhotsk, north of the Kuril island chain and Hokkaido, and east of Sakhalin Island. But there would be one major change to the original plan. He and *Barb* would work with two other submarines, USS *Herring* (SS-233) and USS *Golet* (SS-361). As with *Barb*, both those boats would be commanded by rookie COs. For *Golet*, this would be only the boat's second war patrol since arriving in the Pacific. The three boats were to work as a wolfpack, and Gene Fluckey was to be the commander of the group.

The admiral and his top advisors had recently been moving

more and more toward having submarines attack in closely co-ordinated threesomes. The Germans had demonstrated the effectiveness of such tactics. The relatively new VHF radio systems on US subs made it easier to coordinate with one another. And, for the first time in the war, the US had enough boats in the fleet to make such a ploy possible.

Lockwood looked directly into Fluckey's eyes and asked him, "Can you handle it?"

"No problem, sir."

"Good luck and good hunting," Lockwood told him. With a handshake and a hearty slap on the back, the admiral was gone.

Gene Fluckey had just been wondering if he was going to lose his new command before he even took her to war. Now he was blessed with more command responsibility than he could have ever imagined.

But he was confident. His answer to the admiral had been sincere. He could play the political game as well as anyone, but he knew better than to just tell Uncle Charlie what he wanted to hear.

That included the part about sinking five enemy vessels.

MAY 21

> 1630 *Departed Midway in accordance with CTF 17*
> *Operation Order No. 164-44*

MAY 22

Omitted. Crossed date line.

MAY 23

Commenced daily training consisting of section dives, drills,
fire control drills, enlisted school for qualification, Officers
school for department qualification.

Barb left on schedule on May 21, 1944, along with her two
sister boats. Throughout the run across the Pacific, northwest-
ward toward the far northern reaches of Japan, Eugene Fluckey
continued to train his crew, indoctrinating them into the new
ways of submarine warfare as he expected them to apply it.

He had noted on previous boats that officers usually stood
long and tiring watches. He needed his leaders to be alert and
ready to go at any time. Without consulting anyone, he shortened the lengths of their on-duty time to help keep them fresh
and alert.

Standard operating procedure on subs was that if an aircraft
was spotted, no matter how far away or its direction of travel,
the command to dive the boat was automatic and immediate.
Do not try to determine if the plane had spotted the sub, or
even if it was friend or foe. Dive, go deep, and stay down long
enough to assure the aircraft had left the area. Only then should
the boat come to periscope depth to confirm that there was no
longer a threat. Fluckey had seen far too much of that sort of
duck-and-run on his just-completed PCO trip on *Barb*. Yes, if
the plane was closer than five or six miles, take the boat down.
Fluckey was not crazy. But otherwise, stay topside and keep a
watch on the aircraft. There was a good chance it had not even

spotted the submarine, and would not unless it flew much closer. But should the plane turn toward them, they were not to hesitate. Go to three hundred feet. That seemed to be the best depth, assuming there was three hundred feet of water available in which to hide.

Even if the aircraft appeared to be friendly, they would not stay topside and try to exchange recognition signals. Friends could be just as deadly as foes if they mistook *Barb* for an I-boat. No, promptly dive the boat and live to fight again.

Barb arrived on station in late May 1944. The waters of the Okhotsk Sea typically freeze in the winter and can still have floating ice, even in the summer. *Barb* encountered plenty of ice when they got there. Any man lost overboard would soon perish in the frigid water, likely within twenty minutes. Most bays and harbors offered another hazard. Minefields protected the enemy ships, especially submarines. By the time *Barb* and her wolfpack mates arrived, there was abundant shipping traffic in the area—not just Japanese ships, but Russian ones as well. Russia had still not declared war against Japan and its vessels sailed Empire waters without fear. This reminded some of the holdovers from *Barb*'s Atlantic duty of when they had to be extra sure of the nationality of their targets before shooting.

There were plenty of enemy warships about, though. They seemed determined not to allow access to the Sea of Japan, which lay to the west. And to protect harbors, factories, mines, and other industrial facilities ringing the Sea of Okhotsk. The ships that carried the output of those factories, mines, and forests, too.

When he got a message that a Japanese troop convoy was headed their way, Fluckey attempted to contact the other two boats in the wolfpack. *Herring* answered his summons immediately. No word yet from *Golet*. No time to wait for the straggler. Targets were about to parade right past them like ducks in an arcade shooting gallery.

Barb and *Herring* used their newly installed radar sets, the ones the Japanese could not yet detect, by turning the beams on and off. *Barb* sent a series of Morse code B's. *Herring* responded with the letter *H*. This was a new recognition procedure Fluckey had dreamed up. It worked well. It would soon be employed by other boats in the fleet working together in wolfpacks.

The two subs formed up and made plans, now that they were within sight of each other and communicating bridge to bridge using megaphones. They worked out details on how they would attack together as soon as the convoy appeared on their radar screens and, ultimately, in their periscopes.

Sure enough, right on time, the three troop ships and their lone destroyer escort popped up on radar. Fluckey raced along on the surface to get *Barb* ahead of the ships. As they reached their desired spot and were clearing the bridge, they heard explosions. The sonar operator reported they sounded like the blasts of a ship being struck by torpedoes and then the deep boom of depth charges. Rookie skipper Lieutenant Commander David Zabriskie Jr. on *Herring* had launched his attack already. And it sounded like they were giving the enemy hell. Fluckey later learned that *Herring* had taken out an escort vessel. It was the destroyer *Ishigaki,* whose captain tried to destroy the submarine even as the Japanese ship sank.

Gazing through the periscope, Fluckey could see one of the ships, a troop ship with guns ready, had changed course and was heading straight at *Barb*. He told the team in the conning tower that they would first turn their bow to the approaching vessel and shoot three torpedoes. Then they would spin around and, if needed, launch a spread of torpedoes from the stern tubes, fulfilling a promise he had made to the torpedomen back there. They had complained about not seeing enough action under the previous skipper.

Fluckey coolly watched the target barrel directly toward his periscope. When it drew within 1,400 yards, he issued his first attack command as a sub skipper: "Fire four!" Then, in rapid succession, "Fire five! Fire six!"

Each torpedo nudged *Barb* noticeably as they spun away, flushed out of their tubes by high-pressure compressed air. The weapons quickly accelerated toward the narrow profile of the onrushing troop ship.

It was difficult to tell which was louder, the booming explosion of a solid hit on the target two minutes later or the raucous cheers of the crew up and down *Barb*'s length. Fluckey summed up the result of their work in one sentence.

"We hit directly under her stacks." Perfect shot!

Then, as he watched, there was a second awful blast. Apparently, the ship's magazine—where ammunition is stored on a ship—detonated. That explosion did far more than nudge the submarine. Nobody complained.

Fluckey motioned for each of the attack team in the conning tower to step over to the 'scope and observe their handiwork. They could see, as the target quickly sank, soldiers climbing into landing craft on the deck and floating away. But some of those craft were caught up in the whirlpool, dragged down as the big ship sank. Other men jumped from the doomed ship's decks into the frigid sea and certain death if they were not pulled from the water soon.

Shortly, once the three forward torpedo tubes were reloaded and ready, Fluckey took the boat to the surface. He intended to offer medical assistance to survivors and possibly take a prisoner or two. But as soon as he opened the hatch to the bridge and climbed up, bullets from a machine gun pinged against *Barb*'s hull. The shooting likely came from men in the landing craft. Fluckey went right back down the hatch. And once in the conning tower, the hatch cover above them shut and secured, he ordered the crew to forget the survivors if they were going to shoot at *Barb*. They would go looking for another target.

It did not take them long to spot one. Another troop ship. But it would take more than three hours of negotiating through thick fog to get to a position from which to attempt an attack. Once there, finishing the job took only about three minutes. All three fish from the stern tubes hit the target, breaking her in half. Men in lifeboats who were trying to get off the doomed vessel were spilled into the icy water as what was left of their ship listed violently. After another three minutes or so, the enemy vessel was gone.

Just then, from out of nowhere, an airplane dived on *Barb* and dropped a couple of bombs near them. Very near!

The boat was rocked by both blasts as Fluckey ordered them to go to three hundred feet. Though their teeth had been rattled and most men aboard now had headaches, the close-by explosions had caused no injury or serious damage. But it was an awfully close call.

Later, *Barb* surfaced and surveyed the results of their efforts. The water was littered with bodies floating amid chunks of ice. Some survivors, near death, floated on bits of debris. One man, atop a piece of wood, floated close enough that he was taken as a prisoner. Later, working through the language barrier, they determined that the rescued man had been a lookout on the ship they sank. He was the one who sounded the alarm as he saw *Barb*'s torpedoes racing their way. He also confirmed that a submarine—certainly the *Herring*—had earlier sunk their escort. And his ship had heavily depth-charged the area where they suspected the sub was. The POW had seen no signs that they hit it.

The prisoner was also willing to divulge the locations of mines in La Pérouse Strait should *Barb* decide to go after the other troop ship. Fluckey decided not to do that. He speculated that *Herring* had likely chased the escaping vessel and Zabriskie and his guys had a good head start.

After *Barb*'s hot-and-heavy action, Fluckey allowed his crew to catch their breath. The next morning they celebrated the two sinkings with cake and "medicinal" alcohol. Then they got busy trying to reconnect with *Herring* and finding out where *Golet* might be.

Fluckey later learned he had guessed correctly. *Herring* had, indeed, chased after the last potential target from the convoy. Zabriskie likely suspected the ship had sought safety in the port at Matsuwa Island, in the Kuriles, at the southeast corner of the Sea of Okhotsk. The troop ship was not there, though. Zabriskie spotted two other worthy targets and fired torpedoes, sinking them both. But before the submarine could escape, shore battery gunners observed the wakes of *Herring*'s torpedoes. They drew a bead on their point of origin and blasted away, blowing off the submarine's conning tower.

Herring went down, claiming the lives of all eighty-three men aboard. Her official loss date would be June 1, 1944.

Unaware of the fate of their wolfpack mate, and despite the increasing concern about *Golet*'s tardiness, *Barb* cruised about, looking for something else to shoot. They spied other targets but were unable to launch any attacks. One they almost went after was a great-looking objective, but they realized at the last moment it was a Russian vessel. A poorly marked one. That had become a recurring problem. Fully half the ships spotted on the patrol would be Russian. And Russia was an ally of the US.

Fluckey was keen on using the submarine's deck guns to launch a barrage on one of the smaller ports in the area. But he was reminded that there were either treacherous minefields protecting the harbor or there were air bases in the area. Air response would be quick and deliver much worse than frayed nerves and pounding headaches. The POW also made a point of the danger from those airfields if a gun attack was attempted on the nearby port towns. No reason to doubt him. The former lookout did not wish to go down again, this time on the new ship on which he rode.

Fluckey steamed southeast, to near the Kuril Islands. There was the cable relay station there that he had spotted during their ingress into the Sea of Okhotsk. But they almost ran aground several times because of inaccurate charts. Any attack would be very risky. Even if they got close enough to start shooting, the fog had rolled in, drawing a thick curtain between *Barb* and her target.

Fluckey gave up on the cable station. At least for now. He promised himself that he would return someday and take it out. He was certain its loss would be damaging to the Japanese war effort. It would also be a good example of the shore barrage capability of submarines and their deck guns.

On June 11, *Barb* sighted a potential target on radar. When Fluckey learned what it was, he was reluctant to go blast away at it. A fishing trawler, likely out looking for seals. He did not like the idea of shooting at workingmen braving these inhospitable waters to earn a living for their families. But his orders were to shoot anything Japanese. The fishing boats carried radios, after all. They could well be performing picket duty, looking for and reporting submarines even as they hauled in the catch that would help feed or provide clothing for enemy soldiers and marines—Japanese warriors who would soon be shooting at Americans and their allies.

Fluckey gave the order to chase after the trawler amid huge floating chunks of pack ice and some especially tall frozen mounds resembling icebergs. As it happened, the pursuit and sinking of the fishing boat became one of the more unusual attacks of the war.

JUNE 11, 1944

> 1150 *Manned gun stations. Laid ship 10 yards off the ice field. Commenced firing the 4-inch. An odd practice with the target weaving his way slowly in and out among the bergs. Fired 31 rounds of 4-inch at ranges of 3-4000 yards with many near misses . . .*

1216 *Frankly don't believe we ever got a direct hit but*
shrapnel from the near misses and flying pieces of
ice finally sank the trawler and destroyed
numerous icebergs.

A few hours later, they saw another fishing boat and sank it as well, again using their four-inch deck gun to good effect.

Not long afterward, they spied targets more to Fluckey's liking: a couple of ships carrying military cargo. Between them, they also transported almost four hundred soldiers. *Barb* shot a spray of six torpedoes at the two vessels, hitting both. One was obviously sinking but the other one, though damaged, turned, trying to run away. It lobbed shells in the direction of the submarine. As the sub and its quarry charged back and forth through the phosphorescence of each other's wakes, *Barb* finally had a good firing angle from the aft torpedo tubes. The men back there who had once felt forgotten were now seeing plenty of action, and, in good fighting spirits, they did their part to help blow the ship apart.

All the time, the crew of *Barb* alternately marveled or cringed at their new skipper's unconventional tactics. At one point, Fluckey ordered a crewmember to climb the shears and hang bedsheets. That was to conceal the submarine's dark-metal sail. The boat, on the surface in full daylight, would now blend in better with the white and gray pack ice. It worked as they successfully stalked a target without ever being spotted. However, they were never able to get into a good position from which to take a shot.

Another time, Fluckey precisely mirrored a small convoy's

zigzag course to get a sense of the rhythm of their maneuvering, and to place *Barb* in the perfect spot to take a shot. Of course, as they sat there waiting for one of the ships—an icebreaker—to make its next expected sharp turn, the men in the conning tower realized they were about to be rammed if the target did not zig on schedule. Nothing to worry about. The ship did exactly as Fluckey predicted, driving directly into *Barb*'s crosshairs.

"We were holding our breaths for the expected zig away," Fluckey later wrote in the ship's log. "The bow wave of the target looks tremendous bearing down on us."

The target was hit and, with her whistle blaring for the entire agonizing time, like a painfully wounded animal, the icebreaker sank by the stern.

Shortly afterward, an IJN destroyer showed up, spotted the glow of phosphorescence in *Barb*'s wake, and gave chase. It lasted off and on for the rest of the night. The warship jettisoned almost forty depth charges trying to crush the submarine. At one point, while running on the surface, the ever-resourceful Fluckey told a sailor to fill a gallon milk tin with dirty oil, punch a hole in the top, and heave it over the side. The hope was that the lurking destroyer would see the oil slick in the water and assume their depth bombs had hit home.

That was exactly what happened. *Barb* escaped the wrath of a perfectly capable pursuer.

Though Fluckey had achieved his seemingly impossible promise to Lockwood—*Barb* had already sunk five worthy targets—he still had torpedoes left. Enough time and fuel to look for more ships, too. They passed on shooting at sampans, the small, usually flat-bottomed wooden boats. In the patrol report, there is one full page of times listed for contacts, bearing, radar range, and then the notation: "Sampan. Avoided."

The CO wanted to again attempt to contact both *Herring* and *Golet* so they could conduct at least one coordinated wolf-pack operation to report to Admiral Lockwood. So far, *Golet* had not been heard from at all and *Herring* had not been in touch since she went chasing after the fleeing troop ship.

Just as it was with learning the fate of the *Herring*, Fluckey would not hear about what happened to *Golet* until they returned from the patrol. Under command of new skipper Lieutenant Commander James Clark, *Golet* had run into trouble while passing through the Kuriles on June 14, headed to the rendezvous in the Sea of Okhotsk with Fluckey in *Barb* and Zabriskie in *Herring*. *Golet* never made it that far. According to postwar Japanese records, an antisubmarine patrol intercepted *Golet* off the northern coastline of Hokkaido and promptly sent her to the bottom. Eighty-two men went down with her.

Golet was officially designated as having been sunk on June 14, 1944. Based on the dates declared lost, *Herring* was the thirty-first and *Golet* was the thirty-second submarine lost in World War II. Between the two wolfpack mates, 165 men "went on eternal patrol," the term submariners use when talking about the death of a sub sailor. And with it being the first run for both captains, it certainly contributed evidence to Lockwood's theory that a skipper's first and fifth patrols were the most likely to end badly.

With no rendezvous and low on fuel, *Barb* finally turned east and set out for Midway. They happily celebrated Independence Day twice, on both sides of the international date line, then steamed into Midway on their second Fourth of July.

The commander of Submarine Squadron Four, writing in the second endorsement of *Barb*'s report on her eighth war patrol, made a point of praising the submarine's rookie skipper: "It is noted with pleasure that the new Commanding Officer retained the initiative on all attacks. By so doing, he was able to attain 70% torpedo hits, and in each case effect an expeditious retirement."

Admiral Lockwood's third endorsement to the war patrol report was just as generous in praise for Fluckey and crew: "The eighth war patrol of the BARB was the first for the new commanding officer, as such . . . [T]his patrol was a fine example of outstanding determination, excellent initiative, aggressiveness, and splendid torpedo and gun attacks."

Eugene Fluckey would receive the Navy Cross for his leadership. The citation said, in part, "Skillfully maneuvering his vessel into favorable strike position despite the hazards of adverse weather, ice floes and fog, Commander Fluckey launched torpedo attacks to sink five enemy ships totaling more than 37,000 tons and account for two more in aggressive gun battles. Despite persistent hostile countermeasures, he employed skillful evasive tactics to bring his ship to port without damage. His leadership and devotion to duty reflect the highest credit upon Commander Fluckey and the United States Naval Service."

They had been on patrol for a long fifty-one days. They still had a week's trip ahead of them, on to Pearl Harbor for a refit. They left Midway on July 5. Then came a message that Admiral Lockwood wanted to see Fluckey again when *Barb* was docked and secure in Hawaii.

Based on previous events, Fluckey was wary. Now what? But then he learned that Uncle Charlie had someone who wanted to meet the Navy's newest submarine ace.

That someone was the commander in chief of the armed forces of the United States of America.

CHAPTER TWELVE

"THIS BEAUTIFUL FIGHT"

27 JUNE 1945

> **0822** Two bombs. Close. Just as periscope was being raised for first time in 12 minutes. Evidently our hull is visible against the bottom in such shallow water with a calm sea above us. Raised periscope anyhow to observe formation. TERUTSUKI is leaving formation and giving us a zero angle on the bow at about 7500 yards. Plane overhead. This looks like a nice place to take departure from. Secured attack and commenced evasion.

The words of Commander Eugene B. Fluckey in the report of his twelfth war patrol—his fifth as commanding officer of USS *Barb*—clearly show his frustration. He had already demonstrated his reluctance to withdraw from an attack to evade enemy warships. Now here he was, forced to do just that. All this came after spending two days doggedly tracking a Japanese convoy, a pack of prime targets, as it made its way down the eastern coast of Sakhalin Island in the Sea of Okhotsk. This came after advance notice of the convoy's presence by an unusual atmospheric event that allowed him to see the enemy ships much sooner than would have otherwise been possible.

The convoy they were stalking had suddenly moved closer to land, into water too shallow for the submarine to operate safely. Then the sub's crew realized that one of the convoy's escorts was a newer and very efficient antisubmarine destroyer, a *Terutsuki*-class warship. And that guy was very aware *Barb* was lurking out there. He was perfectly willing to take on the US submersible and end that threat to his flock. He was still four miles away but coming fast, his bow wake resembling a white mustache above an evil smile. To make things even more dicey, there was at least one airplane buzzing around, too, and the pilot would easily be able to see the sub in such clear, calm, shallow water.

To add to Fluckey's frustration, *Barb* had fired a new, experimental acoustic-sensing torpedo at the destroyer the day before. It was a dud. Duds could be deadly for the warship that fired them.

Even so, Fluckey decided the convoy was ripe for the taking. He still had plenty of the older-type torpedoes, which were performing much better now that Admiral Lockwood had convinced the Navy to fix them. Additionally, Lockwood had also authorized his captains to modify them as they saw fit. The skipper ordered the crew to "battle stations, torpedo," to come to periscope depth, and be ready to finally launch an attack on those prime targets they had been watching for so long.

Once he raised the periscope, he immediately spotted their two sources of potential trouble: the destroyer and the aircraft.

Two blasts suddenly rocked the submarine viciously, giving every man a severe jolt.

"Dive! Dive!" The klaxon sounded as they promptly assumed a sharp down angle.

They would have to hurry—or at least go as fast as they could while submerged—to deeper water. It was now clear the aircraft could see them very well—see them and guide the destroyer skipper so that he could drop depth charges to maximum effect. BOOM! BOOM! Two more bombs exploded, shaking dust and insulation loose, knocking men off their feet.

"Rig for depth charges!"

0825 *Two bombs. Close.*

0832 *Depth charge distant.*

0833 *Depth charge distant.*

0855 *Two depth charges to port. Fairly close.*

0900 *Twenty six fathoms.*

0900 *Two depth charges to port and ahead.*

0904 *Two depth charges to port. Decided to open coast, surface and end around to a point south of KAIHYO TO where we would have 30 to 40 fathoms to attack in.*

The depth charges from the destroyer were giving them a pummeling and certainly shattering some nerves. But now they

were past a hundred feet in depth, so the airplane could probably no longer see them. The destroyer, though, had apparently
drawn a good bead on them with their sonar. The blasts appeared to be getting closer.

Then Fluckey and his crew found help in the form of water
temperature at one depth being much different from that at another. Such a variance caused a deflection of the sonar sound
waves from the enemy warship and ruined the attacker's aim.
Barb's sonarman reported the explosions were becoming less accurate. The destroyer had lost them—at least for the time being.

Deeper water. That was what *Barb* needed. The convoy had
come up with a very effective defense. The submarine could not
attack from the west. That was land over there, narrow as it was,
offering the ships a solid shield from that direction. They were
almost always in shallow water, too close to the coastline for
Barb to come at them from that direction. The antisubmarine
destroyer and the patrolling aircraft kept Fluckey in deeper water but out of range. Even if they got past those two and close
enough to attack, there were other, perfectly capable frigates, a
couple of other antisubmarine patrol vessels, and likely depth
bombs and guns on the freighters—and more warplanes where
that one came from.

Most captains would have steered away to safer waters, then
look for something easier to shoot at. The crew of *Barb* had
served under their skipper long enough by now to know such a
capitulation would never even occur to him. He ordered a course
that mirrored the convoy's. When it was dark enough, they
came to the surface to try to get ahead of them. The moon and
good weather were not their friends. They had to keep a sharp

eye from the bridge and lookout platforms for aircraft or approaching ships, as well as from the conning tower, using the broader view the height and magnification of the periscope provided.

When the sun was appearing as a dim glow in the east, they dived once more, back to hiding. At one point, they remained uncharacteristically submerged for almost eighteen hours. The captain gave the order to limit smoking among the crew to preserve fresh air. He might not have bothered. The oxygen in the submarine grew so sparse that matches would not strike. And even if they did, cigarettes refused to stay lit. Even more serious, lights were growing dimmer throughout the boat. Anything not essential that used battery power was turned off. Coffee grew cold in pots. Meals consisted of anything that did not require cooking.

When they finally surfaced in the darkness on the night of June 28, all hatches were thrown open. The chill sea air never smelled so sweet. A battery charge was started. Men in the shears kept an especially sharp eye on the sky and horizon.

Fluckey dubbed this a wasted day. But he knew it would be worth it if he could finally hem up that damned convoy and start shooting. Their chances of doing that now depended on where the ships were bound. The captain was reasonably sure the caravan had anchored just inside Patience Bay, near Kaihyo Island, and, as usual, in water just deep enough to keep their keels out of the mud. If they were headed to the port at Shikuka, they would remain close to shore all the way around the bay to the ship channel there. There would be nothing Fluckey and his crew could do. *Barb*'s time pursuing the convoy, from a shimmering mirage at the horizon all the way to Patience Bay, would have been one colossal and perilous waste. But if the procession was bound elsewhere, farther down Sakhalin Island, the north coast of Hokkaido, the Kuriles, or through La Pérouse Strait, they would have to soon come out and swim in deep water.

Deep water would allow *Barb* to do what she wanted. Still dangerous with those air and sea escorts, but at least a fighting chance.

Finally, on the morning of June 29, *Barb* swung around into Patience Bay to come at the convoy from the west and try to determine where the targets might be headed. The sub remained mostly at periscope depth, hoping no aircraft could see them. Once, with the sun almost directly overhead, Fluckey raised the 'scope, took a quick look, slammed the handles back down, and ordered a dive.

"Rig for depth charge!" he called out. He had spotted a pontoon patrol plane only two hundred yards away at ninety degrees off their port. It was flying only fifty feet above the wavetops. Close enough that Fluckey could clearly see the pilot's face.

No way he had not spotted the submarine!

Amazingly, he had not. The plane flew on south, maybe in the direction the convoy would be heading shortly.

Sure enough, about forty-five minutes later, Fluckey was peering through the 'scope again when he sang out, "Man battle stations, torpedo! Here they come!"

No doubt it was the same convoy. Lord knows they had been

looking at it long enough to recognize it. But Fluckey noted a change. One frigate was gone. He would keep that in the back of his mind in case the treacherous warship suddenly appeared from nowhere at an inopportune time. The newer destroyer was still there and visible, though, just as ugly and menacing as ever, running south out of Patience Bay at a range of nine thousand yards. An airplane was up there, too. It was about halfway between the submarine and the gaggle of smoking ships now coming into view from the shallow water, close enough that the pilot may have already spotted *Barb* at periscope depth. But maybe not. For the time being, the plane was weaving back and forth in front of the destroyer, watching for the submarine they suspected was still out there somewhere, lying in wait for the convoy.

Gene Fluckey made a quick decision. Getting a shot at the other ships would be far easier if he eliminated the threat of the *Terutsuki*. Otherwise, that vessel was going to keep the sub at a distance. Fluckey was going to take on the warship, even if it required a down-the-throat shot, a torpedo fired at the destroyer's bow as it steamed straight toward the sub. That meant firing torpedoes at a very narrow target. There was a distance problem with that, too. If *Barb* fired torpedoes too soon, the destroyer could easily see them coming and simply dodge them. If they shot too late, the fish would not have time to arm themselves, meaning that even if they hit dead-on, they would not explode. Also, it would give the submarine very little time to dodge the oncoming warship and they might well be rammed. The destroyer would win that kind of collision.

The first torpedo shot was one of the acoustic homing

torpedoes loaded in tube ten. It performed exactly as the previous one had: thirty seconds or so out of the tube, it disappeared. The destroyer was still headed their way, making good speed. Not exploding and going up in flames as the *Barb* intended.

Fluckey ordered a slight turn to port to have some angle on the *Terutsuki*. Not quite a dead-ahead shot. But while they maneuvered, the patrol aircraft must have spotted them.

1307–1309 *FIVE bombs. Dust and cork flying. Periscope acting like a whip antenna.*

1317 *Target speed 10—knots pinging. Range 1700 yards, angle on bow 5 starboard.*

1318 *Depth charge.*

1319 *Explosion or depth charge.*

1320 *TORPEDO ATTACK 1A.*

The bombs fell much too close for comfort. A fine dust filled the air in the compartments on the submarine. Anything not tied down rattled around inside the ship. Now, with the destroyer coming at them at ten knots, and with the attacker inside a thousand yards' range, and since they could see a sliver of the starboard side of the deadly warship, Fluckey ordered tubes seven, eight, and nine fired.

All three conventional torpedoes ran right at the target, perfectly aimed. They missed. The destroyer had suddenly slowed, just enough to cause the torpedoes to go harmlessly past.

Fluckey popped the 'scope back up, just above the sea surface. No sign of the airplane. Suppose he had dropped all the bombs he had? It had certainly felt like it. But the enemy warship was now almost on top of them. Down 'scope!

Fluckey told the crew in the conning tower to forget the airplane. Worry about the destroyer. And for good reason. The thing was plowing right over them, narrowly missing them.

> 1324 *TERUTSUKI passing overhead. Screws clearly audible.*

> 1325 *Eight Depth charges. Ahead, above and below mostly to port. Raised scope to see a continuous stream of depth charges coming out of his side throwers. A thrilling sight with the ship doing a ST. VITUS dance and ST picking up the geysers from the depth charge explosions.*

> 1327 *Six or more depth charges. Terrible TERUTSUKI now turning and coming back with plane doing figure eights just forward of his bridge.*

> 1331 *TORPEDO ATTACK #1B.*

The plane was back. That was not the biggest problem. The destroyer had made a U-turn. Another down-the-throat shot would offer only a narrow-angle view of the attacker's starboard side to shoot at.

Fluckey requested a sounding. They had just over a hundred

feet of water beneath them. Tight. Not nearly enough to go deep after taking another shot at the destroyer.

Three shots, to be precise. And they had better hit.

A quick look through the 'scope: The target was where she was supposed to be, closing fast. Three more conventional electrical fish sped away from *Barb*. Sonar reported they were "hot, straight, and normal," headed straight for the destroyer on their preset course and at their assigned depth.

Meanwhile, as they timed the torpedoes, Fluckey ordered, "All ahead, full, for twenty seconds. Then all stop."

That maneuver would create a swirl of water, called a "knuckle" by mariners. The bubbles it created would hopefully give the destroyer's sonarman plenty of noise to concentrate on while *Barb* ran away.

Then came the maddening update.

"All three fish missed," sonar reported. "Sounded like they ran under the target."

Fluckey could not believe it. Lined up perfectly, set to run at six feet deep, and aimed at a target the skipper was certain would draw at least fifteen feet of water. Yet their torpedoes had passed harmlessly beneath the destroyer's keel. There was no time to pitch a fit. Or try to figure out what happened.

"Close all watertight doors except the hatch from the conning tower to the control room," the captain ordered. "And hold on to something solid."

Depth charge explosions erupted all around them. The destroyer passed them once again. This time over the spot where they had left the swirl of water with the "all ahead, full" command. Still too close, though.

Fluckey refused to give up. He lined up and fired the last of the experimental acoustic torpedoes, designed to home in on the sound of a ship's screws. At the moment, that sound was substantial.

Just as happened twice before, sonar lost any noise from the weapon about thirty seconds into its run. Despite all the booming and shaking, one of the officers had the presence of mind to express the opinion that the cold water might be having some effect on the sophisticated devices. They had only been tested in Hawaii, and in Narragansett Bay at Newport, Rhode Island, in late spring. Not in water with patches of ice floating all about.

To the dismay of some of the crew, the captain pressed on. Once the destroyer was past them again, despite the almost continual booming of the detonating "ash cans"—slang for depth charges—he raised the 'scope and got a reading on the range, bearing, and speed of the target. Three more torpedoes whooshed away. *Barb*'s crew hardly noticed the kick as the compressed air shoved the weapons out of their tubes. They were being rocked too hard by the depth charges. But with the target only six hundred yards away, they would soon know if they had finally managed to hit him.

"Torpedoes all passed directly under the vessel and continued on the same bearing. Now fading out."

"Damn the torpedoes," Fluckey said, but with little emotion. "All ahead full for twenty seconds." A twenty-second pause. "All back, emergency." Then: "Take her down to eighty feet."

Again, Fluckey was creating a minor maelstrom in the waters, stopping, starting, dashing from one course to another, all to confuse the sonarman on the IJN vessel about exactly what was a submarine and what was not. Then, when their newly installed depth charge direction indicator confirmed the Japanese vessel was dropping their ash cans ahead of where the sub was, the skipper ordered, "All stop. Rig ship for silent running."

If those guys did not know where *Barb* was by now, they were no longer going to give them any help finding her. After the next round of depth bombs, already far too many to tally, Fluckey ordered them to proceed at one-third speed. To leave the area.

They still had to keep an eye toward the nearby beach and be constantly sounding to assure there was water beneath them. At the same time, he asked his officers to eject every evasion device they carried. Anything that would make noise somewhere *Barb* no longer was. And hope that would be enough commotion and chaos to allow them to escape this debacle.

1333–34 *Ten or more depth charges to starboard and astern, above and below. Released 5 NAC beacons set on 3 minutes delay at about one minute intervals. Threw a couple of full speed knuckles then slowed to 70 RPM and withdrew tactically and tacitly from the coast. Several escorts made sweeps around us occasionally but never picked us up again.*

1450 *Periscope depth. DD and a DE still searching well astern of us.*

1615 *Bomb—distant.*

1950 *All clear. Sun still up. Surfaced, plotting all kinds of foul deeds. The convoy has gone by. It is probable that they will spend the 4 hours of darkness at AIRO WAN then on through LA PEROUSE. Much to our disgust we lack two hours of being able to hop in the ring with the TERUTSUKI for a fifth round.*

Fluckey would later write in his patrol report, "Consider ourselves extremely unfortunate to only get a draw in this beautiful fight after all the punches we threw."

A disappointed Fluckey ordered a full inspection of all remaining torpedoes and their fire control system, from the torpedo data computer all the way to the tubes themselves. They had that destroyer dead to rights several times but the weapons in *Barb*'s holster failed them. That was no way to bring a speedy end to this war.

Meanwhile, the captain began having conversations with his officers about those foul deeds he had in mind. He desperately wanted to strike a blow against the enemy that the IJN would long remember and to accomplish something that further proved the value of and need for submarines in this and future sea wars. Plus, if it made everybody in the Silent Service marvel at what *Barb* got done, then that would be all the better.

For starters, he wanted to go back to the port where the convoy on which they had just whiffed had come together. There might be other ships there now. Maybe another full convoy emerging from the harbor into open water. He also had an idea about hitting a seal rookery and radio station he had spotted along the eastern shore of Sakhalin, near the entrance to Patience Bay. That was while they were wasting their time stalking the luckiest convoy in the history of naval warfare. With a little ingenuity, he believed they could wreck the place, which was likely a worthy target in its own right. Seal oil was a natural resource the Empire needed. Sealskins were used for jackets for pilots and other warriors. Fluckey felt that they could also get a prisoner and possibly even capture documentation about upcoming ship traffic in the Okhotsk Sea. That would be a useful guide to what and where to attack. A smorgasbord of targets.

There were some other objectives he wanted to hit with their deck guns. Still others he felt were perfectly suited for an assault using the rockets now that he and his crew had learned to use them more effectively.

Then there was the other potential target upon which he had been cogitating ever since *Barb*'s last visit to the Okhotsk Sea on her eighth run. A hit on a type of target never struck by a submarine. This one, he knew, could be taken out with no worries about malfunctioning torpedoes. He only needed to come up with a plan.

As they left their frustrations behind at the mouth of Patience Bay, the CO needed to decide—with input from his wardroom—which one of these unorthodox assaults he and his enthusiastic but tired and disappointed crew should attempt first. Tactics he had been dreaming of since before the war, back on the old *S-42*.

While serving on the old problem boat *Bonita*.

And ever since he had successfully removed the stain of the "problem boat" label from the USS *Barb*.

CHAPTER THIRTEEN

BACK TO SCHOOL

Eugene Fluckey felt he had gotten excellent on-the-job schooling during his two and a half years of service on USS *S-42* in Submarine Division 11 out of Coco Solo, Panama. It had not been easy duty, though. Habitability aboard the old boat was lacking. She tended to break down often, so a tender typically was close by while the boat was on maneuvers around the Caribbean and Gulf of Mexico. Though *S-42* was one of the later submarines in the class, she was still getting long in the tooth when Fluckey came aboard for his first duty in the Silent Service at the end of 1938. But he saw this as a good opportunity to learn every nuance of this decidedly different kind of vessel.

How they worked. How to keep them working. How to dive and surface under all kinds of conditions.

They conducted many, many drills stalking destroyers and

other friendly vessels, and got plenty of practice ducking and dodging aircraft. He soaked up every aspect of service aboard submarines and remained convinced this was where he wanted to spend his naval career, and was similarly convinced that he could get even more out of this old boat if he were her CO. Then do truly remarkable things with the newer boats once they were afloat.

The young submarine officer almost got himself seriously injured once when he inadvertently stepped backward, unaware the deck grid had been moved for some maintenance. He fell hard into the boat's bilges. Though he got a nasty cut on his leg and plenty of bruises all over, he somehow avoided broken bones. Or worse.

Fluckey enjoyed those times when the boat would rest motionless on a calm sea in tropical waters, allowing the crew to take a leisurely swim. It was a bit unnerving to have sailors with rifles in the shears to watch for sharks. There was also the redhead's proclivity for sunburn. He wrote Marjorie that "I am as red as a spanked fanny. A few more freckles will probably be the outcome."

The most disappointing aspect of his time on *S-42* was not being able to spend as much time as he expected with his wife and baby daughter. While he was learning all he could about submarines, his girls were back in Coco Solo, the town originally built to house the workers who dug the canal. Marjorie kept busy with Barbara and other Navy wives, and she and her husband wrote letters to each other almost every day when apart, letters that would typically not be exchanged until Gene was already back home for a precious few days of leave.

Then came the short-lived move for the family back to New London, the disenchantment of not getting the sub command Fluckey expected, the reassignment to *Bonita* back in Panama in June 1941, and the planned reuniting of the little family for Christmas that year, abruptly sidetracked by war. Gene's prediction that the conflict would not even last the three months until Barbara's birthday in March was proven wrong when the day came and went. Yet he remained aboard *Bonita*, still learning but now actively defending, and with his girls back up north in Connecticut, awaiting the first blooms of spring.

Fluckey continued to try to put the best face on things in his letters. "I feel that your being in New London is for the best—it's so much safer there and you are free from the cause of the jitters the families down here seem to have had lately since being sand-bagged and blacked out."

There remained well-founded concern the canal would be a Japanese target. But the newly promoted full lieutenant Fluckey was even more convinced that *Bonita*'s second through fifth war patrols—from January through the middle of May—were doing very little to help end the war. Patrol reports for each run contained a litany of complaints about a lack of contacts and continued mechanical issues with their ship. He had decided that there was little left for him to learn from the old boat and there would be no opportunity to put into practice some of the tactics he longed to try. About the only excitement on those runs was dodging US aircraft whose pilots had become trigger-happy in anticipation of Japanese and German submarines in the area. If *Bonita* went down, it would likely be from friendly fire, not in a running gunfight with a U-boat.

There was still no sign that he was even under consideration for his own command. This despite the need for aggressive submarine skippers to helm the new subs that were already seeing plenty of action around the Pacific. Boats on which he could prove not only their value but his.

That was when Fluckey made a fateful decision, one that bothered him mightily and could have kept him from ever commanding a submarine. He applied to a postgraduate design engineering degree program that required that he study for a year at the US Naval Academy in Annapolis and then two more years at the Massachusetts Institute of Technology in Cambridge. Fluckey worried that some would think he was taking this step to avoid going to war. Two things convinced him to take this risky course and submit his application. First, when he checked the list of fellow submariners who had undertaken this program of study, he noticed that almost every one of them had become commanding officers.

The second was more personal. If he were accepted, he would spend the next three years with Marjorie and Barbara Ann and not far from the rest of his family. Worries about his wife's diabetes continued to weigh heavily on Fluckey. He was always concerned about whether she was getting the correct dosage of insulin and following her strict dietary requirements. It would not take much of an error to be fatal. Gene believed he was the best person to assure that did not happen.

In June of 1942, shortly after arriving back in Panama from *Bonita*'s fifth war patrol, he received permission to start school. Reunited with his family, Gene went right to work cracking the books, beginning midsummer in Annapolis. However, he never really expected to be in the classroom for the next three years. He kept an eye on the war and what was happening with submarines. What he saw gave him hope he would soon be pulled from school and put on the bridge of a submersible. Marjorie's mother was placed on alert to be prepared. Should Gene suddenly get sent to the Pacific, she would have to come to Annapolis and move in with her daughter and granddaughter. She was a registered nurse and familiar with Marjorie's diabetic needs. She had sometimes stayed with them when the family was previously separated.

Submarine losses were mounting. So far in 1942 the *S-36* (SS-141) (ran aground and scuttled), the *Shark* (SS-174), the *Perch* (SS-176) (scuttled, crew taken as POWs), the *S-27* (SS-132) (ran aground and abandoned), and the *Grunion* (SS-216) had already been damaged, declared missing, or gone down, taking the lives of hundreds of qualified submariners. There were other problems, too. Skippers who had taken command between the wars were unable or unwilling to run their boats as aggressively as their higher-ups felt was necessary. But unit commanders were reluctant to replace them with newer COs who might put the limited fleet of subs and their crews at too much risk. There was also the continuing problem with dud torpedoes, an issue that had become a scandal and was costing lives.

Any day now, Fluckey thought. Any day the call would come, and he would finally get his command.

Summer waned. Fall in Annapolis was golden. Fluckey hardly noticed as the leaves eventually fell and then snow covered the beautiful and historic Naval Academy campus. Spring of 1943 came and went with no summons. Then, just as he was preparing to relocate his little family to the Boston area and continue his studies at MIT, orders appeared from out of the blue.

All his lobbying had finally paid off.

Gene Fluckey was to report to New London for submarine Prospective Commanding Officers' School. Someone had finally noticed that potentially one of the best sub commanders in the Navy was trying to maintain an *A* average in engineering design down at the Academy. Now he was to start his new curriculum in November 1943.

After talking it over, he and Marjorie decided that she and Barbara would remain in Annapolis, and Marjorie's mother came to stay as long as she was needed. PCO school would take about five months. After completion, Gene would be headed to the Pacific.

The curriculum was a breeze for Fluckey. He had learned most of it already serving on the two boats in the Caribbean and Pacific around Panama. There was new material on even newer boats that were now fighting the war, but it all made perfect, practical sense to him. The PCO students routinely received war patrol reports from the real world, just off the mimeo machines in Hawaii. Gene devoured every one of them, fascinated by the daring but canny tricks the best skippers employed. Men like Dudley "Mush" Morton, Dick O'Kane, Sam Dealey, and Fluckey's Annapolis classmate Slade Cutter. He was also fascinated by their colorful and descriptive writing style. Their patrol reports often read like dime novels.

The exploits of one skipper were especially interesting to Fluckey. That was Lawson "Red" Ramage, another redhead who almost missed becoming a submariner because of vision issues.

Ramage injured an eye while competing in wrestling at the Academy, but he memorized the eye chart and got through. Ramage's aggressive tactics as skipper of USS *Parche* (SS-384) would earn him a Medal of Honor. He was the first living submariner to receive the award.

It was early spring of 1944 when Fluckey received orders to report to the submarine base at Pearl Harbor, Hawaii. Though he hated to once again kiss his girls goodbye, he was excited to know he would likely be on patrol, heading his new command, within a month or so. But fate had still more frustration awaiting the eager PCO.

Because he had spent all his submarine service thus far down there in Panama, and that had been on the old, outdated S-boat and the rickety V-boat with the misspelled name, the Pacific Fleet submarine commander assumed Fluckey was still not ready to command one of the *Gato* or *Balao* boats. Instead of immediately taking out one of those subs, Fluckey would be assigned to work on the busy sub tender anchored there in the harbor, welcoming in the submarines as they returned from war patrols. He could put to good use his engineering studies by helping oversee and improve maintenance procedures. He would be learning what had worked and what had not, reading every word of the war patrol reports to see how the current crop of captains were doing things, well, badly, or indifferently. That would give him a better idea of how to captain those sophisticated boats.

That was not Fluckey's expectation when he headed out to Hawaii. It was especially galling that, at age thirty, he was already one of the senior PCOs at Pearl. But the Navy was about to have him spend his time inspecting flanges and valves and pipes, reading mostly dull, boring, self-promoting war patrol reports.

"How long will it take?" Fluckey asked his boss. "How long before I get my own boat?"

"A couple of months, maybe" was the nebulous reply.

Though it made no sense to him, Gene Fluckey was bound to do what his superiors told him to do. He would be the best welcomer and refit overseer the US Navy had ever seen. The best thing that could happen would be the war would be over and won before he became a CO. The next best thing would be that he would get his boat, go out there, and help defeat the Japanese.

He was assigned a cabin on the submarine tender, moved in, and planned to get up and go to work each day. He shared his exasperation in letters to Marjorie and Barbara. Fluckey only hoped the poor guy who had to read and censor his mail did not get tired of all the whining about his predicament.

Then, after his first day on his new job, there was that knock on his cabin door at two a.m.

Fluckey and another girl with the same name as his daughter were about to finally meet for the first time.

CHAPTER FOURTEEN

A THREE-RING CIRCUS

The turnaround between USS *Barb*'s eighth and ninth war patrols would not be as quick as Gene Fluckey wanted. But it would be eventful. After departing Midway Atoll on July 5, 1944, they arrived in Pearl Harbor on July 9 for a two-week refit. That two weeks would turn into three, as *Barb* would not be ready for sea until August 4. It did offer much-needed leave for the crew. Most of them were staying at the Royal Hawaiian Hotel, the luxury accommodations the Navy had turned into a prime R&R spot for submariners while in port.

Nobody was upset about that except the skipper. He was anxious to get back to the war.

There was also the matter of the previously issued summons from Admiral Lockwood. The admiral had someone who wanted to meet his new star skipper. It was not just *Barb*'s remarkably successful eighth patrol and Fluckey's audacious leadership style that had made him stand out from the rest of the submarine action. His patrol report for the latest run had been written in a highly entertaining style and colorfully recounted not only the attacks but also the unusual sights and events encountered along the way.

Lockwood had forwarded the patrol report to Admiral Chester Nimitz, the commander of the Pacific Fleet. Nimitz enjoyed it so much, and was so markedly impressed, he passed it along to the commander in chief of the US military, President Franklin D. Roosevelt. The president read it on his way to Pearl Harbor for a meeting with Nimitz and General Douglas MacArthur, officially Supreme Commander, Allied Forces, Southwest Pacific. When Roosevelt learned that the submarine skipper who had written that report and run his ship so aggressively would coincidentally be in port, he asked to meet him.

That meeting took place on the street in front of the Royal Hawaiian. A big black limousine rolled to a stop at the curb as Fluckey and Lockwood waited in the shade of a palm tree. Lockwood opened the rear door of the car to reveal three of the most powerful men in the world at the time: Nimitz, MacArthur, and the president of the United States.

Roosevelt's prime interest was in why the *Barb* was only submerged for a single day out of the total of fifty-two days of the patrol. That was not his understanding of how submarines operated. Fluckey explained that this was based on very simple geometry. While submerged at periscope depth, whoever was on the 'scope could only see about a dozen square miles of ocean, and then only if the sea was calm enough. On the surface, with the 'scope fully raised and its magnification engaged, he could then see more than two hundred square miles. Fluckey also reminded the president that the difference in capable speed while submerged and when on the surface enabled the submarine to cover far more territory and locate targets.

The president told Fluckey he could sleep better knowing that men like the skipper were out there taking the war to the enemy. He also requested that Lockwood and his staff forward each of *Barb*'s patrol reports to him as soon as the boat returned from each run. He wanted to continue closely following the exploits of the submarine and her captain.

The men exchanged salutes, the door was closed, and the big limo drove away down Kalakaua Avenue. Fluckey shook Lockwood's hand, thanked him for the honor, then went back to his letter-writing. He told Marjorie about the incident but assumed his dealings with the president were over.

That was not the case. The next day, an aide to Lockwood informed Fluckey that the president wanted to take movies of *Barb* re-creating her return from the just-completed patrol, passing a viewing stand at Pearl Harbor, so he could show everyone back in Washington the submarine that had so impressed him. Fluckey was not enthusiastic about such a thing. This would take time away from the refit. Plus, he would have to pull crewmembers away from their R&R to power up and navigate past the president. But for the good of *Barb* specifically and the submarine service generally, he agreed to do as the president asked.

Roosevelt was not happy with the first run past him. The sub was going too slow. The impressive pennants in the shears hardly moved at all. The president requested another trip.

When Admiral Lockwood personally told Fluckey to do it again but much faster, the skipper almost blew a fuse. Pearl Harbor was busy, filled with vessels, many moving about. The area *Barb* was transiting for the president's film camera was cramped. A full-speed run was dangerous. The risk of damaging the vessel was real. That would even further delay their departure for war patrol number nine.

But if Roosevelt wanted a show, *Barb* would give him a show.

"All ahead full!" Fluckey ordered. Smoke poured from the boat as she surged ahead, racing past the president, pennants flying. Lockwood looked on and held his breath. The sub was about to crash into a nearby pier.

At the last instant, Fluckey ordered, "All back, emergency! Left full rudder!" More black smoke and an eruption of water from *Barb*'s screws. The boat shivered. Somehow, though, she eased to a stop only a few yards from the pier and catastrophe. Crewmen moored her right there, ready to continue repairs.

President Roosevelt had gotten just the film footage he wanted. And in the process, Fluckey had successfully demonstrated not only the capabilities of his submarine, but also those of the crew and captain of USS *Barb*.

The ninth patrol was to be another wolfpack run, with *Barb* this time working with USS *Tunny* and USS *Queenfish* (SS-393). Also riding along on *Barb* was Captain Edwin Swinburne, who had been serving as Admiral Lockwood's flag secretary. He would be the commander of the wolfpack even though he had never made a war patrol in a submarine. He did have ten years' experience in the boats prior to the war, though. Still experimenting, Lockwood had a notion that it was asking too

Eugene B. Fluckey, captain of USS *Barb* (SS-220).

USS *Barb* on patrol in the Pacific.

Barb at Mare Island Naval Yard, California, just prior to departure for her historic twelfth war patrol, spring 1945.

Gene Fluckey on the bridge of *Barb*, lookouts in the shears.

ABOVE: On the deck of *Barb*, Fluckey wears the Navy Cross medal he has just received. Note the sub's insignia on the boat's fairwater behind him.

LEFT: Midshipman Eugene Fluckey, from the US Naval Academy yearbook, *The Lucky Bag*.

Stern view of *Barb* at Mare Island Navy Yard preparing for her twelfth and final war patrol.

Medal of Honor presentation ceremony for Gene Fluckey in Washington, DC, March 1945. From left, Fleet Admiral Ernest J. King, Secretary of the Navy James Forrestal, Fluckey and his wife, Marjorie, and Commander and Mrs. Roy M. Davenport. Davenport, also a submarine skipper, received one of his five Navy Crosses at the event.

The crew of *Barb* rescue Australian and British POWs. The ship on which the prisoners were being held was sunk by a US submarine, which was unaware there were POWs aboard.

Out of torpedoes and shells on her twelfth patrol, *Barb* resorts to ramming an enemy trawler to sink the vessel.

The infamous *Barb* battle flag upon conclusion of her final WWII patrol. In Pearl Harbor in August 1945, the men holding the flag made up the demolition team that went ashore and blew up a train in Japanese-held territory. From left to right: Chief Gunners Mate Paul G. Saunders, Electrician's Mate 3rd Class Billy R. Hatfield, Signalman 2nd Class Neal Sever, Ship's Cook 1st Class Lawrence W. Newland, Torpedoman's Mate 3rd Class Edward W. Klinglesmith, Motor Machinist's Mate 2nd Class James E. Richard, Motor Machinist's Mate 1st Class John Markuson, and Lieutenant William M. Walker.

Note on the *Barb* battle flag the unique patches along the bottom for rocket attacks and the assault on a train.

After becoming a part of the Italian Navy, *Barb* was renamed the *Enrico Tazzoli* (S 511), here shown in Genoa, Italy, in 1956.

After the war, Fluckey served as an aide to Admiral Chester Nimitz.

Eugene Fluckey retired from the US Navy in 1972, having achieved the rank of rear admiral.

much of the skippers in the wolfpack boats to also command the group.

The three submarines would have the advantage this time of conducting practice with one another while making the trip from Pearl Harbor to Midway, "attacking" their escort destroyer. That had not been the case with *Golet* and *Herring*. Also, once again, the captains of the other two boats—Elliott Loughlin in *Queenfish* and George Pierce in *Tunny*—were making their first runs as COs. Fluckey was the experienced one with a total of one war patrol on his command résumé. But the "old-timer" knew Loughlin from back at Annapolis. Loughlin was actually older, two classes ahead, and was named the top athlete his senior year of '33. Based on that, Fluckey was certain he would be a good teammate. He did not know Pierce but had heard good things. With the opportunity to impress Swinburne, who was only one step removed from Lockwood, and with two promising partners on the other two boats in the wolfpack, Fluckey felt positive about his second run as CO of *Barb*. He hoped for a bountiful hunting ground.

Though Lockwood offered Fluckey the opportunity to return to the Sea of Okhotsk, he turned it down. He did want to go back there at some point, but only when he would have the opportunity to try some new things and take along some new equipment he had been thinking about. The destination for the wolfpack this run—they were already nicknamed "Ed's Eradicators," after Swinburne—turned out to be the Luzon Strait, a narrow body of water between Formosa (Taiwan) and the northernmost Philippine island of Luzon. It was now the busiest shipping channel for the Japanese and promised plenty of potential targets. However, enemy convoys in the area were well protected by aircraft from nearby bases, destroyers, and other warships.

Ed's Eradicators maintained a "scouting line" twenty miles apart as they steamed toward the strait. Fluckey pondered a knotty dilemma as they pounded westward. Edwin Swinburne had a reputation as a stickler for rules and regulations. Fluckey was intending to take on plenty of beer to reward his boys after they did great things out there. He was afraid Swinburne would object, pulling rank. But once they were at Midway, at a dinner hosted by the sub base commander there, Fluckey learned naval regulations allowed a ship to carry a half case of beer per man, ostensibly for picnics. He left the dinner long enough to phone the boat and tell the on-watch officer to go requisition the suds, but the officer reported that they simply did not have enough room to store it. *Barb* was full.

"Put it in the officers' shower," Fluckey ordered. That would be the incentive for his officers to sink ships. Only when the beer was gone could they take a shower.

Once they passed through the strait and were in the South China Sea, the three subs were to meet up with another three-boat wolfpack and proceed to sink anything that floated and flew the "meatball" flag of Japan. When *Barb* began passage through Luzon Strait on August 21, all they saw were other US submarines and occasional enemy patrol planes. Then, nine days later, after doing nothing but diving to avoid bomber airplanes, they received a message that the code breakers had learned about a big convoy coming their way, well escorted, from Formosa and headed to Manila.

AUGUST 31

0120 *Surface patrolling on scouting line. Sighted smoke. Commenced tracking. Received contact report from QUEENFISH. Picked up three other sources of SJ radar interference. This area being unassigned is open hunting for any wolfpack. The Busters* must have just arrived. Looks like a three ring circus is about to start with two wolfpacks and one convoy.*

0130 *Proceeding to position as starboard flanker.*

0143 *SJ radar contact on convoy at 18000 yards. Also on a night flier coming in fast. The show has started. Curtain time. Dived.*

When Fluckey took his first look through the periscope at the approaching convoy, he immediately sent instructions to remove four cases of beer from the officers' shower and place them in the freezer, but there were anxious moments ahead. As he lined up for an initial attack, one of two torpedoes from the *Growler* raced just above *Barb*—one of the hazards of operating in a wolfpack! Both of the torpedoes went on to strike a tanker. It sank immediately amid billowing black smoke. But all that smoke, fire, and noise alerted the convoy that they were being shot at. They quickly executed a radical zig. If Fluckey wanted

---

* Named for its commander, Benjamin Oakley, "Busters" was Ben's Busters, the other three-boat wolfpack on the scene: USS *Growler* [SS-215], USS *Pompanito* [SS-383], and USS *Sealion II* [SS-315].

to shoot and hit anything, he would have to again get into a prime position.

That was just one of the skills that made Fluckey so revered by his crew and so admired by his commanders. He had a knack for keeping a mental picture of all that was happening on the surface as well as below it, where every ship and submarine was located, and the speed, range, and firing angles necessary for getting in position to shoot at the best and most enticing targets. It was a game of quick-moving, three-dimensional chess, and Fluckey played it as well as anyone—even if the competition was shooting real bullets and dropping actual TNT.

0230–0238 *About 25 assorted depth charges and bombs.*

0240 *Surfaced. Determined to introduce another character into the plot. End of ACT I.*

0242 *AIRCRAFT CONTACT #12. Sighted plane 3 miles astern after another sub. Did not dive.*

0245 *Requested enemy position from TUNNY who was port flanker. Burning tanker had now sunk. Water surface still ablaze.*

0305 *AIRCRAFT CONTACT #13. SJ radar contact on plane at 8650 yards. Slowed and turned away. Did not dive.*

Submerging while a monster convoy was in sight, even if the radar screens showed aircraft nearby, was not an option.

They could never catch up if they ducked to hide from those planes.

Now the skipper brought *Barb* into position—"a position which has been my dream," Fluckey later wrote—to fire three torpedoes at a freighter and a tanker that were running very close together. If he were lucky, or if his calculations were correct, two of the fish would hit the initial target while the third would strike the big tanker that was a few hundred yards closer but to the right of the freighter. "It was too good to be true," he later wrote. However, there was another chilling moment when he spotted a torpedo from one of the other subs. It was on the opposite side of the convoy. It was zooming straight toward *Barb*. With Commander Swinburne looking over his shoulder, Fluckey calmly lowered the periscope. The fish swam right on past without taking a bite.

The wolfpack commander peeked through the 'scope at the mayhem his boats had caused. Several other ships, including one of the escort destroyers, were afire and sinking.

With the sun now up, the convoy was apparently hurrying back in the direction from which they came, toward Takao on Formosa. The surviving ships were not visible but the swarm of aircraft guarding them buzzed overhead like bees.

0735 *Up for look. Remains of convoy hull down now headed west with 8 planes covering . . . a vicious circle for the Japs. The convoys bring gasoline and bombs for the planes to sink the subs which sink the ships which bring the gasoline and bombs for the planes etc.*

0920 *Convoy had now given up trying to make the Philippines and was now disappearing to the North towards TAKAO.*

1250 *No further smoke. Gave up high speed and set course to south west clearing area. End of ACT II.*

Much later, Fluckey learned that the tanker his torpedo had hit made it back to dry dock on Formosa. It would take three months at best to get her back in service. Later, it was determined that the damaged vessel would have to be moved to a bigger yard farther north. During that transit, a temporary patch covering the hole *Barb*'s torpedo inflicted in its hull failed. The ship ran aground. There she stayed the rest of the war. *Barb* and Fluckey never got recognition for the loss. Postwar records gave credit for the tanker to Allied aircraft, though there is no record of any plane ever shooting at the vessel while she was still afloat. The hulk attracted plenty of target practice, though.

That August day's show was not quite over yet, even if much of the cast had left the stage. For a curtain call, Fluckey and his crew launched an attack on what appeared to be a small transport ship and two escorts, all well armed and dangerous. Another factor was that, with all the morning's action, *Barb*'s batteries were ominously depleted.

Then a pesky bird landed on the attack periscope, his tail feathers making it impossible to see what they were shooting at. The fowl refused to move, no matter how much banging and up-and-down movement the attack officer on the sub did to the 'scope. Fluckey would later call the bird "the latest fiendish anti-submarine weapon of the Japs."

It ultimately took the bright flash and ear-splitting explosions of *Barb*'s torpedoes hitting the transport to shoo the bird away. The torpedoes split the ship in half, just as Fluckey realized what he was shooting at was not a transport at all. It was a disguised gunship, part of a "hunter killer" group, sent in response to the wolfpack's earlier attack on the convoy.

Whatever she was, she was no longer a threat. But her escorts certainly were. They raced over to the vicinity from which *Barb* had fired and began dropping depth charges—fifty-eight in all.

Barb was better than three hundred feet deep by then and headed away from the spot. Though the continual explosions rocked them hard, there were no injuries or damage. They were a safer five miles away before they could surface and charge the batteries. Without their juice, there would be no safe way to dive. They would be easy pickings on the surface.

The nearby enemy airfields proved to be a continuing issue. Fluckey was also becoming suspicious that the Japanese were somehow detecting the submarine's SJ radar and using it on moonlit nights to get the drop on them. They were constantly harassed by bombers. Once, they spotted a plane that suddenly appeared on the horizon. *Barb* dived and Fluckey watched the bomber race directly overhead past them. The pilot seemed to ignore the sub, though. Then Fluckey realized it was headed straight for the position of the *Tunny*. The skipper tried to warn his sister boat to go deep.

There was no reply. Repeated calls resulted in no acknowledgment. There were only the booms of distant bombs exploding.

Fluckey watched through the periscope as the plane continued to bomb his sister boat. At one point, he saw *Tunny*'s stern go high out of the water. A bomb had almost certainly exploded close beneath her.

Fluckey and Swinburne feared the worst, but there was no time for worry—only for silent prayers.

About midnight, *Barb* was on the surface when radar showed another aircraft racing at them. They submerged, but the roar of the plane's engines was so close and raucous that they woke Gene Fluckey from a sound sleep. As he came running into the control room in his skivvies, a close bomb blast rocked the sub. Then three more. One close blast broke bulbs and filled the air with cork dust, paint flakes, and insulation, spiderwebbing gauge glass and sending sailors flying. The submarine continued to dive on down to the usual hiding depth, below three hundred feet, the vessel's test depth. (Beyond three hundred feet deep, the sub was no longer considered to be watertight and safe from the massive pressure of seawater.)

Again, no one was hurt, though nerves were on edge. Damage was minimal. Later, when they surfaced, they found pieces of a bomb fin and other shrapnel impaled into the teak decking and tangled with topside parts of the boat. It had been an even closer call for *Barb* than they had realized.

The captain deemed it a good time to break out the ice-cold beer and celebrate the sinking of the hunter-killer ship the day before. That would help settle the crew's nerves.

After two more days of worry, Swinburne and Fluckey finally heard from USS *Tunny*. She had survived the bombing but suffered heavy damage. Though she could dive, the four aft torpedo tubes were out of service and her rudder was not working well. Her dive depth was severely limited. She was unable to report her survival because her radio antennas had been blown off. *Tunny*'s crew rigged a makeshift aerial so they could report in. Swinburne ordered her back to Midway.

The rest of August and the first two weeks of September were spent mostly hiding from aircraft. They were up and down so much, one of the officers asked why they even bothered closing the hatch cover from the bridge to the conning tower, and bombed so often Ed Swinburne quipped, "We need to go to Saipan to reload, not torpedoes but light bulbs."

In mid-September, *Pompanito* and *Growler* sank several Japanese troop transport ships in the South China Sea. That was almost five hundred miles from *Barb* and the other boats in the group. Afterward, the subs realized that many of the thousand or so survivors in the water were British and Australian prisoners of war. *Pompanito* and *Growler* picked up as many of them as they could, about 130 men. But that was all they could hold. *Queenfish* and *Barb* raced that way to try to save more lives. As they ran along at top speed, the crew tried to make room for up to a hundred weak and famished men, hoping all the time they could fill the space with rescuees.

Then something got in *Barb*'s way: a large convoy, a mere 150 miles from where the survivors were in the water.

They decided to take time to do some damage before hurrying on to their rescue mission. *Queenfish* fired her last four torpedoes left aboard and took out a tanker. The ships altered course and all Fluckey and his crew could get lined up on was a trailing tanker.

But then lookouts on *Barb* saw something else lurking in the middle of the convoy. Something very big. Fluckey could not believe his luck.

SEPT. 16

2325   *Ye Gods, a flat top! This was the large pip about 300 yds to port and just ahead of the very large after tanker in the starboard column.*

2328   *. . . this is undoubtedly the prettiest target I've ever seen . . .*

It was an aircraft carrier. The *Unyo.* One of the most sought-after targets in the Imperial Japanese Navy. And *Barb* and *Queen-fish* had simply happened upon her and the heavily laden tankers while going somewhere else. But the escort destroyers—one a *Chidori*-class torpedo boat, an especially dangerous adversary—were already aware of the two submarines and were racing at each of them at top speed, depth charges racked and ready.

Almost in a single breath, Fluckey ordered the firing of all six torpedoes that were loaded in the forward tubes and for the boat to go deep. Just before he put the periscope down, he could see one of their torpedoes broach, running up and down, in and out of the water on the surface. It would be unlikely to hit anything. Hopefully all the information entered into the sub's torpedo data computer was accurate. Prayers went up that neither the tanker nor the aircraft carrier would be able to veer too much from their original course and dodge the half dozen torpedoes headed in their direction.

But whatever happened, *Barb* would not be there to watch. They were headed deep and with a full-right rudder the instant the last torpedo spun away from its bow tube.

After the quick shoot-and-dive, they braced for the expected depth charging. It never came. The torpedo boat had apparently not seen them before they went deep.

2334-16 *First hit in tanker.*

2334-24 *Second hit in tanker.*

2334-53 *First hit in carrier. Chidori passing overhead.*

2335-01 *Second hit in carrier.*

2335-10 *Third hit in carrier. No depth charges. The Chidori must not have seen us.*

2337-2345 *Breaking up noises, very heavy underwater explosions, whistlings, cracklings. One ship sunk. Random depth charges started.*

It would be an hour later before *Barb* risked poking her periscope above water. They could see what was left of the convoy, including the *Unyo*. Men were trying to save the ship as escorts buzzed all around, occasionally launching some depth charges but mostly pulling survivors out of the sea. Before the convoy was even out of sight, and with little chance of launching another attack, the two submarines hurried on toward the poor POWs trying to survive in the South China Sea.

Despite the efforts of her crew, *Unyo* would sink within six hours, well before she could reach land.

When *Barb* and *Queenfish* reached the spot where the troop transports had sunk, they found a grisly sight. Swollen bodies floated everywhere. The stench was awful. They found a few men in rafts or swimming in debris, barely alive. They continued searching, finding a man here and another there, determined to get as many as possible, even when the wind picked up and the seas became dangerously rough; "in the tail of a typhoon," Fluckey would term it. Some *Barb* and *Queenfish* sailors had to jump into the roiling sea to get to survivors and then swim back to their subs.

Crewmembers on deck and the bridge had to tie themselves to something solid to avoid being washed overboard in the storm. Soon they could find no more survivors. The next day, as the weather improved, they only saw bits of wood and debris. Anyone who had managed to survive to that point had been washed into the sea during the night.

In all, *Barb* had picked up fourteen men and *Queenfish* eighteen. Not nearly the one hundred each for which they had prepared space.

The two submarines set a course for the nearest US-held territory, Saipan, in the Mariana Islands. Once there, the crew of *Barb* took up a collection to give to their rescued survivors. Practically every cent on board, almost $300, went into the kitty.

Gene Fluckey would later write, as an addendum to the report of *Barb*'s ninth war patrol: "The appreciation of the survivors was unbounded. Even those who couldn't talk expressed themselves tearfully through their glazed oil soaked eyes." Fluckey recommended special commendation for *Barb*'s pharmacist's mate, William Donnelly. He had worked day and night to care for the rescued men on the run to Saipan and, because of his skill and dedication and despite their terrible physical condition, every one of the men pulled from the water survived. Donnelly would be awarded the Navy and Marine Corps Medal.

Queenfish lost two of the men they had pulled from the water, both of whom had been unconscious when rescued. Both received burial at sea, ejected from the boat's torpedo tubes.

Barb arrived in Saipan on September 25. In addition to sending the survivors ashore, they picked up one torpedo to go along with the five they had left. They also took on twenty thousand gallons of diesel fuel. The Navy and Commander Swinburne still had things for the two remaining boats of Ed's Eradicators to do on this run. They first headed to Majuro in the Marshall Islands, where a sizable Navy base had been constructed. There the crew could enjoy a few days of swimming and sunbathing. However, there was little else to do in that out-of-the-way enclave.

Plans were to detour the wolfpack while they were on the way to Majuro so they could launch a barrage on the Japanese-held Wake Island. That order was canceled by the submarine force honchos back at Pearl Harbor with no reason given to Swinburne or the two submarines' captains. Instead, they continued to Majuro. There, the patrol mostly faded to an end in the stifling heat, cloying humidity, and incessant bugs of that distant outpost. The men slept in steamy Quonset huts and ate food from cans. But at least—despite occasional air raid alerts—nobody was shooting at them or dropping depth bombs on their heads. Their mail caught up with them, too, including a stack of letters from Marjorie to Gene.

Ultimately, after two weeks in the Marshalls, *Barb*'s tenth patrol would launch from there.

Fluckey would be two for two, receiving his second Navy Cross for his second run as captain of *Barb*. The medal citation summed up the reasons: "Pursuing aggressive and tenacious tactics despite strong countermeasures by the enemy, Commander Fluckey launched damaging torpedo attacks against Japanese shipping and combatant units to sink a 10,000-ton auxiliary aircraft carrier and to damage a tanker of 5,000 tons. Effecting the rescue of fourteen British and Australian prisoners of war who were survivors of a torpedoed enemy transport, he provided care and treatment for the sick and wounded and, although heavy enemy counterattacks caused minor damage to his ship, employed evasive tactics and returned to port without further damage."

Barb's skipper was also promoted from lieutenant commander to the rank of commander.

The submarine force soon received messages of appreciation from the British Joint Staff, the Australian prime minister, and even Sir Winston Churchill. They acknowledged just how dangerous the effort to rescue the POWs in a typhoon and enemy waters had been.

Perhaps the highest praise for *Barb*'s skipper and crew came from Admiral Lockwood. In his endorsement of the ninth patrol report, he succinctly wrote, "This patrol is a continuation of the illustrious record of the BARB." Later in the endorsement, Lockwood wrote, "The spirit, determination and coolness displayed, along with the tender care given the rescued nationals of our Allies are in keeping with the splendid record already established by the BARB."

As it turned out, Uncle Charlie had not seen anything yet.

CHAPTER FIFTEEN

MISSION OF MERCY OR MURDER

Despite the need for R&R and the initial tropical beauty of the place, nobody on USS *Barb* wanted to remain at Majuro Atoll any longer than necessary. Not even if it meant heading right back out on war patrol, the submarine's tenth. That included her skipper, about to make his third run as *Barb*'s commanding officer. Eugene Fluckey would later write, "On an all-male island there was little to do except write letters— no natives, no athletic fields, no movies, little reading material, and poor swimming, for the beach was steep and loaded with sandflies."

Fluckey had taken advantage of the lack of distractions to continue training the crew. At least that kept their minds off the heat and sandflies. "With the limited facilities available, training was thoroughly conducted, ably planned, and well-coordinated," he later wrote in the final report of *Barb*'s tenth war patrol. "Convoy College was held on the beach, and night and day convoy exercises were held using anything that had a pair of oars."

"Convoy College" was the term the submarine COs had coined for their wolfpack practice and strategy sessions anytime they were together in one place with nobody shooting at them. If Fluckey was going to operate with partners, he was determined that they would all be doing the same dance. Otherwise, it could be downright dangerous when all three submarines, plus other packs in the area, were shooting at targets at the same time in the same patch of ocean. On this run, *Barb* would be operating again with *Queenfish* with Elliott Loughlin still in command, and with a new partner, USS *Picuda* (SS-382), whose new CO was Tyler Shepard, yet another Annapolis classmate of Fluckey's. *Picuda* would be making her fourth war patrol.

Fluckey was once again pleased with the territory they were assigned. They would operate in the East China Sea, south of Korea and off the coast of the southernmost Japanese Home Island of Kyushu. That would put them in the vicinity of major enemy naval bases at Sasebo and Nagasaki. Targets should be plentiful. But so would mines and patrol boats and sneaky-quick aircraft.

Before they left, Fluckey dropped a stack of letters to Marjorie into the bag bound for the censor. He had so far told his wife fairy tales about what was going on, never alluding to his having seen any action at all on his first three runs as CO. He made a point of never mentioning him or the boat being in any particular danger. He had almost run out of made-up excuses for lack of combat. In fact, the censor would have likely blacked out such comments anyway, but he did not want her to worry.

He also wondered if she was telling him the whole truth in her letters to him about her own physical condition. Or did she not want to worry him, either? She had shared in one letter that she had fallen into a diabetic coma on a couple of occasions, once when only Barbara Ann, who was now seven years old, was there with her. She had given her mother orange juice and candy to bring her out of it. But, she maintained, everything was under control now and he was not to worry about her. Gene could only hope his fiction was more far-fetched than his wife's.

With Elliott Laughlin in *Queenfish* specified as the wolf-pack's commander, they dubbed themselves "Laughlin's Loopers." The plan was to stop in Saipan just long enough to top off with diesel fuel, then continue. Each boat would operate independently until one or the other spotted a convoy worthy of convening the wolfpack. Then they would all conduct a well-coordinated attack on the targets.

They left Majuro behind on October 27, 1944, arrived at Saipan in the Marianas on November 1, and departed about eight a.m. the next day. The submarines arrived on station on November 6. Two days later, Fluckey once again had the opportunity to turn a problem into a solution.

Barb was patrolling near a major naval air base on Fukue Shima, one that protected the harbor at Nagasaki to the east and the factories and military facilities at Sasebo to the northeast of the island. The sub was shrouded by a blinding rainstorm. But suddenly, as they ran on the surface, the rain squall blew away, leaving *Barb* exposed in broad daylight in a busy tub of water. Most skippers would have pulled the plug and gone deep to lessen the chance of being spotted. Not Eugene Fluckey.

He told a disbelieving crew that, since there were no aircraft in the sky at the moment, and no patrol craft nearby, they would just continue to steam along slowly on the surface and hope that the enemy saw them. If and when somebody showed up, they would then dive. Otherwise, *Barb* would continue to meander southward until nightfall. Then, in darkness, they would make a top-speed run to the other side of Fukue Shima and set up along the busy shipping route from the Sea of Japan into Nagasaki. Meanwhile, the Japanese would be looking to the south, the direction in which that slow-moving submarine had been spotted foolishly patrolling on the surface in daylight.

It took a while, but the subterfuge worked. No one came after them. Then, with the coastline completely dark, lights out as usual to protect against air attacks from the Allies, the big lighthouse at Koshiki suddenly blinked on. Something, most likely an important ship of some kind—important enough that it could not risk remaining outside the harbor until daylight—was approaching the ship channel, requiring illumination to avoid running aground in relatively rough seas.

Barb was waiting. The first shot hit the *Gokoku Maru*, a cruiser, but she still managed to limp away, trying to make it to the bay and safety. Then, after several of *Barb*'s torpedoes ran erratically, missing the target, another one hit solidly, sending the big vessel—10,400 tons and a truly valuable warship—to the bottom. That came at just after four in the morning. Even as at least one patrol boat sped their way, *Barb* remained on the surface and fled the scene, heading north, in the direction of Korea.

Shortly, when dawn came and they felt it prudent to go deep, they could still hear the distant, constant thumps of depth bombs, plenty of them, churning the strait near where the submarine had done its work.

Years later, Fluckey would learn from Japanese naval records that the cruiser was in transit up from Formosa to undergo repairs in the IJN navy yard at Sasebo. The previous day, with reports of the sighting of an American submarine emerging from a rainstorm and patrolling southbound on the surface, *Gokoku* was hastily rerouted, sent toward the port by the northern route, just to be safe.

Even though his plan had worked perfectly, Fluckey was disappointed. The attack had cost him six torpedoes, leaving him with only eighteen. He and his boat had pulled right up to within five hundred yards for the last—and fatal—shot. Two of the fish had run erratically. A third broached and, as Fluckey wrote, "went off into the night." Blame it on the rough seas or whatever, those were six fewer weapons his submarine had to expend now. Fluckey was convinced he would need those and more over the next three or four weeks.

On November 11, *Queenfish* spotted a sizable convoy. After reporting it to his fellow wolfpack members, Elliott Loughlin attacked, taking down one freighter before escorts drove him deep.

Meanwhile, Fluckey and *Barb*, who had been doing lifeguard duty that night for a massive B-29 bomb run, hurried to a point where they could intercept the convoy. They also learned only one American bomber had been shot down during the raid, and that the survivors of the downed airplane and the enemy convoy were conveniently on the same course heading.

NOVEMBER 11, 1944

1505 *Received word of downed plane 170 miles distant.*

1506 *Received word from QUEENFISH of convoy*
she contacted at 0900 forty miles south of us
heading on course 260 degrees, the same general
direction as downed plane. Decided to combine
mission of mercy with mission of murder.
We are now 70 miles behind convoy. Bent on four
engines and poured on the coal.

When they caught up with the Japanese convoy, the biggest question was which of the targets to go after first. There were eleven ships with at least four escorts. But the primary problem was the weather: high winds and seas at force six with fifteen-foot waves. Fluckey and the others on the bridge of the boat had to tie themselves to something solid to avoid being washed overboard. Many of the crewmen below were violently seasick.

There was nothing they could do about the rough seas. Fluckey decided to shoot not at a particular ship but into the nest of them. He would have to hit something. Within five minutes, *Barb* sent six torpedoes into a concentration of cargo ships. Some torpedoes ran an erratic, zigzag course, but Fluckey saw two strike home and explode on two different ships. He was certain at least one of the vessels was sinking and the other was heavily damaged. The rest were scattering wildly, heading off in different directions. The escorts scurried about, trying to determine the compass heading of their attackers.

After a quick reload and spin around to shoot from the stern tubes, one of the freighters ran right behind them at a range of less than five hundred yards. *Barb* launched two torpedoes. Both struck home. The 4,800-ton *Naruo Maru* was a goner.

Fluckey was sure they had now sunk two ships and damaged a third. But he was not satisfied. *Barb* continued to stalk scattered members of the convoy. Not long before the rise of a full moon, they spied another freighter. It would be a tough attack, though. The seas were so rough that it was difficult for crewmembers to safely move the torpedoes around on the skids and get them loaded into the tubes. They weighed more than a ton and a half each. Sea spray and rain made the periscope almost useless. With the sub at periscope depth, the waves also vaulted the boat above the surface at times and dragged them well below periscope depth at others. Depth control was near impossible. The submarine needed to get as close to the target as they could to be sure they were shooting at something that was where they were telling the torpedo data computer it was.

Finally: "Fire eight! Fire nine! Fire ten!"

"All running hot, straight and . . ." BOOM!

Many in the boat thought a depth bomb had exploded right on top of them. The engine room even reported they feared the stern of the boat had been hit.

No. The first torpedo had hit the freighter. It had not taken long at all. A run just far enough that the torpedo had time to arm itself.

BOOM! Another rattling blast. Likely a hit on a second ship they had briefly seen beyond the primary target.

Later, Fluckey would describe the initial jarring blast, saying, "First torpedo hit in forward hold and target blew up in my face, literally disintegrating. Parts of the target commenced falling on top of us, drumming on the superstructure."

Not bad for shooting blindly in the middle of a raging storm with towering waves. He was also confident he heard two vessels breaking up and eventually coming to a crunching halt at the bottom of the sea. There were also sounds of high-speed screws overhead: escort destroyers looking to give Fluckey and his crew a severe headache.

The captain took his sub deeper—to 180 feet, despite the charts and their own soundings showing that they barely had fifteen to twenty feet of water under them at that depth—but he continued to circle beneath the floating jetsam, and below survivors in the water from their last victim. Fluckey reasoned that not even the Imperial Japanese Navy would drop depth charges into the middle of their own flailing countrymen. The Australian and British POWs from *Barb's* last run had reported that when their ship was sunk, the Japanese warships did not launch depth bombs if they might erupt among their own. But they had not hesitated to do so among the POWs in the water. Many of them died that way.

Fluckey's gambit worked for a bit. However, the water was so shallow, he was afraid they were going to have their screws hit the bottom. That would make noise and give away their position. So would using compressed air to blow enough water out of the tanks to rise up a few feet to get them out of the mud. Either way, they needed to do something. The skipper ordered them to come up to a depth of 175 feet.

Click. Boom! The first depth charge rattled the boat. Every man aboard could hear the loud, metallic click of the device as it armed. Then, a half second later, the deafening blast. A bull-dozer ramming full speed into the hull of the submarine.

Another close explosion, obviously set to blow at 175 feet, precisely where *Barb* was resting. It missed by only fifty feet or so.

Then another series of ominous splashes in the water. More depth charges. Everyone held his breath, waiting for the shock waves and ear-numbing blasts—and, maybe, inrushing seawater through a rent in their hull.

Nothing. Nothing but silence, save for the whirling screws of the escort still zooming around directly above them.

"Captain, sonar reporting a bunch of thuds from below us."

Fluckey grinned.

"For once, being in shallow water has worked in our favor, boys. They're setting the detonators for more than two hundred feet to try get one under us. They're settling on the bottom before the triggers are deep enough to activate."

As the submarine eased away, still dangerously near the bottom, they could hear more distant explosions, deeper thunder than that from the depth charges, members of another wolf-pack taking their own toll on the convoy. When *Barb* surfaced, by then ten miles away, they saw the eruption and fire as another ship took a hit from an American submarine's torpedo.

After a battery charge, and with dawn just coming visible in the eastern sky, Fluckey took them down. Everybody was spent from the night's frantic action. They did not even take time to splice the main brace.

Over the next few days, Fluckey and his crew found little action. Then, early on the fourteenth, they saw something else to shoot at. Only a couple of schooners, probably a hundred tons each. But they were Japanese ships and therefore targets.

NOVEMBER 14, 1944

0741 *Manned battle stations, guns.*

0747 *Lookout spotted a plane heading in. It just couldn't be, not at such a critical time. CO finally found reported plane and identified as a bird.*

They ran between the two boats and quickly dispatched both to the seafloor with the submarine's deck guns. A half hour later, another unfortunate schooner popped into view. That vessel soon met the same fate as the other pair.

The next day passed quietly. Then, just before midnight, *Queenfish* and elements of another wolfpack reported a small convoy with a big target speeding directly toward *Barb*'s position. The others were chasing. *Barb* would intercept.

Fluckey knew immediately when he saw it that the big vessel was an aircraft carrier, surrounded by four escort ships, and moving very fast. He also realized that in racing to get to a good firing point, they were shooting spray high into the moonlit sky. They had to slow to avoid getting themselves spotted. But if they could decode the zigzag pattern the five warships were following, they could better line up for a potential attack. It was a complicated bit of submarine geometry.

In the process, *Barb* identified the carrier as the new *Katsuragi*, which had only been launched in January. So far, the vessel had never been out of Japanese waters nor had she yet been loaded with aircraft. Fluckey was determined to make sure neither event would ever take place. When he had good range and angle, he fired their last five torpedoes at the carrier from the forward tubes. All of them were headed directly toward the target.

Then the carrier made a sharp turn. No!

As they watched from the bridge of *Barb*, one of the torpedoes just hit the carrier's stern. The other four flew right past, eventually running out of fuel and settling harmlessly to the seafloor. They could only hope the lone glancing hit would slow the big target enough so one of the other subs could catch up and do far more serious damage.

But if the flat top slowed, it was only marginally. None of the boats was ever able to get a shot. One by one, they called off the chase. The frustrating mathematics of a submarine attack had once again prevented success, no matter how smart or determined the effort had been conducted.

"At dawn we submerged for the morning to rest on our defoliated laurels," Fluckey would later write. The biggest target the boat had seen in her history had somehow managed to run off and hide from them. The other subs, too. And there would be no credit at all for *Barb*'s one hit on the ship.

(It is probable that Fluckey and his crew misidentified the carrier. It was almost certainly the carrier *Jinyo*, also known to be in those waters at the time, at which they were firing. It would have been little consolation to Fluckey and his disappointed crew, but *Jinyo* was sunk by sister submarine USS *Spadefish* two days later. There is no way to know if *Barb*'s torpedo damage to the carrier helped *Spadefish* in her successful stalking and attack.)

With only two torpedoes left, and both those in the stern tubes, there was no point plying the waters near Sasebo and Nagasaki. Instead, Fluckey took his boat south, along the coast of Kyushu, looking for something they could sink with only two fish, or a target worthy of a surface attack. They soon identified two small freighters silhouetted against the shore. They fired both torpedoes, one at each ship. Both missed. One torpedo did make it to the beach and exploded there. The only damage from Barb's attack was to the good night's rest of the inhabitants of the houses clearly visible along the shoreline.

And that was it. A promising run had ended with little to cheer about.

Barb would claim credit for sinking three schooners, four freighters, and a light cruiser and hurting the carrier and two other ships for a total of seventy thousand tons sunk and damaged. JANAC would eventually call it only two ships for 15,200 tons. Either way, by Barb and Fluckey standards, it was a disheartening run, especially considering the prime hunting grounds to which they had been assigned and the capable team members with whom they were working.

There were also worries about Fluckey's executive officer, the second in command, Lieutenant Jim Lanier. During the patrol, he had suffered chest pains. The pharmacist's mate diagnosed him with a heart attack. Lanier spent the last two weeks of the patrol in his bunk but felt well enough to help plot the course back home. Once there, he was sent by air to the naval hospital on Guam. Jim Webster came aboard as Barb's XO for her final two war patrols.

Given the choice of heading for Midway or Pearl Harbor for a refit, the CO chose Midway. Pearl Harbor had a considerable backlog, which would certainly delay the start of the submarine's eleventh patrol. That was not acceptable to Fluckey. He wanted to get back to bringing a conclusion to the war as quickly as he could. He still had plenty to prove.

But not even he could have known just how extraordinary that next patrol—indeed, the next two runs—would be.

★ CHAPTER SIXTEEN ★

"A SPEEDY, DARTING, KNIFE-THRUST ATTACK"

19 DEC. (1944)

> 1430   Departed Midway. Commenced training program
> for officers and men, daily dives and fire control
> party drills. En route Guam or Saipan.

20 DEC. Omitted.

21 DEC. Crossed international date line.

25 DEC. Sank floating mine with twin 20mm. Expended two
magazines. Celebrated Christmas with carols and festivities.

Christmas 1944 came a day early for the crew of USS *Barb*, thanks to that imaginary boundary that demarcates one calendar day from the next, the international date line. It also found them well on their way to a quick stopover somewhere in the Mariana Islands before plowing ahead for war patrol number eleven for the submarine and number four for her CO, Commander Eugene Fluckey.

The skipper had much to ponder as he and his officers put

the boat's crew through their paces over the six calendar days it took them to get to their intermediate stop. That turned out to be Guam. The endorsements to his patrol report for the tenth run were all glowing, but Fluckey was concerned they had expended every torpedo they could carry in just eight days. Though the total count of ships sunk was impressive, he felt it should have been higher. His bosses seemed perfectly pleased. Fluckey expected more of the boat, the crew, and himself.

Secondly, during the time the boat was undergoing a refit in Midway, Fluckey had flown to Pearl Harbor for a sit-down with various members of the submarine command staff. They assured him that *Barb*'s next run would be to the hottest area in the Pacific, the waters of the Formosa Strait and the southern areas of the East China Sea. The Japanese assumed that the Allies were about to make a massive attack on the Philippines to regain the rest of the country. Troops had already taken control of the island of Leyte and were coming ashore on Mindoro while Fluckey was getting briefed in Pearl. The enemy would be doing everything they could to reinforce their troops in the Philippines and prepare them to defend the territory—and invaluable natural resources—they had claimed earlier in the war. That would mean many ships in the water, steaming south, loaded with troops and war matériel. *Barb* and her wolfpack partners were going to attempt to throw down a gauntlet across the Formosa Strait and make sure none of them got to the Philippines. Fluckey was ecstatic.

(Indeed, in mid-January 1945, with *Barb* and the wolfpack doing damage in the strait, about 175,000 men of the US Sixth

Army went ashore on the main Philippine island of Luzon. It would soon become the largest invasion force of the Pacific War.)

But then the skipper got some disconcerting news. His fourth run as a submarine commander would likely be his last.

The psychiatrists had convinced everyone who counted that no CO should make a fifth patrol without a long rest. Once the boat returned from this run, Fluckey was to be pulled from *Barb* to join Admiral Lockwood's staff. Fluckey was furious.

The first person to mention the upcoming reassignment to Fluckey—and the same one who gave him the good news about the eleventh run's operational territory—was Captain Richard Voge, who held a unique place in submarine history. He had been the skipper of USS *Sealion* (SS-195), the first of the fifty-two US boats that would ultimately be lost in the war. *Sealion* was undergoing an overhaul at the Cavite Naval Yard in the Philippines when she was hit by Japanese bombs three days after the attack on Pearl Harbor. Four crewmen died, becoming the first of the more than 3,500 American submariners to lose their lives in World War II.

Voge looked Fluckey straight in the eye and said, "Gene, give up the idea of a fifth run."

Then Admiral Lockwood told him the same thing, and even more forcefully. True to his nature, Fluckey launched into his best sales pitch.

Eventually, Lockwood surrendered. At least partially. He agreed to take into consideration how Gene's fourth run played out. Then, if the Navy docs agreed, Lockwood would consider allowing Fluckey a "graduation patrol." After that, should he survive the run, Gene would absolutely be joining Lockwood's staff.

"Thanks, Admiral. Aloha!"

As Fluckey flew back to join his boat at Midway, another harsh reality hit him. It had now been almost a full year since he had seen Marjorie. She and Barbara had remained in the little cottage in Annapolis where they lived while Gene attended graduate school at the Academy. Now, in only a few days, another Christmas would pass with the family far apart. Another reason, he decided, to do all he could do to try to bring this damn war to a close.

Indeed, as *Barb*, *Queenfish*, and *Picuda* plied the Pacific toward Formosa and mainland China, Fluckey made an optimistic entry in the log at midnight, January 1, 1945: "Celebrated the advent of what we hope is the final year of the war."

That afternoon, *Barb* came upon a three-hundred-ton vessel that had already been worked over by her two wolfpack mates but had not sunk. Fluckey approved an unusual action for a submarine: he sent over a boarding party. Though some of the Japanese vessel's crew were possibly still alive, maybe hiding out in the bilges, the men from *Barb* conducted what their skipper termed a "burglary." They swiped some interesting and possibly useful items from the damaged vessel. That included updated charts, always of value. Then, with one blast from the four-inch gun, they finished what their sister boats had started.

Barb had her first kill of her eleventh war patrol. Or, as it would eventually be credited, one-third of a sinking. That fraction would always be on *Barb*'s record, even after JANAC's postwar reductions. It was an excuse to splice the main brace with champagne that had been placed in the cooler. Fluckey had decided to forgo the bubbly on New Year's Eve. Instead, they would wait for the celebration of their initial sinking, not only the first of the eleventh patrol but of 1945 as well. Though most of the sailors would have preferred the usual cold beer, they still happily toasted to the new year.

By this time, Fluckey and the other skippers were learning new tactics being employed by the Japanese to try to avoid the destruction wrought by the submarines. Ships now tended to stay close to shore, in waters deemed too shallow for the subs to operate. In many places in the China Sea, the twenty-fathom curve extended a good twenty miles out. (A fathom equaling six feet, this meant water depth was less than 120 feet to at least twenty miles from shore. *Barb* required about half of that to run at periscope depth.) The Japanese relied on aircraft to cover the closer-in routes and required fewer escorts, because they only needed them on the seaward side. No submarine could approach a convoy from dry land, of course. To help with air support, the freighters, troop ships, and tankers only ran in daylight, then put into ports along the Chinese coast to ride out the hours of darkness. That was when the subs prowled. Ports were conveniently located at intervals of about twelve hours' travel. It was similar to what *Barb* had encountered while stalking convoys on previous patrols. It was now working well for even more enemy shipping.

As usual, Gene Fluckey had been studying the situation. He had grown a bit tired of the nickname Lucky Fluckey. He maintained luck had little to do with *Barb*'s success. He preferred calling it "serendipity," a more descriptive term that just happened to not rhyme with "Fluckey." Yes, it was good to have luck on their side. But planning, skill, training, and aggressiveness were what it ultimately took to excel, as well as Fluckey's ace in the hole: being willing and able to do the unexpected. Put it all together and you had serendipity, which became one of Fluckey's favorite words.

Now, with the targets hugging the coast, it was another opportunity for the skipper to improvise. He asked the wolfpack commander—once again Elliott Loughlin in *Queenfish*—if he could have the position in the group that would put Fluckey nearest the coast. Since *Barb*'s older sail could easily be mistaken for a fishing junk, and since those craft were floating everywhere in the area, that made sense. It also, as Fluckey intended, put the 220-boat in prime position to spot a sizable convoy. They were coming out of Shanghai for a daytime scramble across the strait to the north end of Formosa. There it could dash on toward the Philippines in daylight the next day.

It was dangerous territory. Not only was it well patrolled, but intelligence confirmed there were more than fifteen thousand Japanese mines in this area, some of which was still designated as "blind bombing zones," meaning Allied aircraft could bomb any vessel they spotted without first trying to ascertain if it was a US submarine. There were also two other US wolfpacks plying the seas around there. One mistake by any of the nine boats, or even a torpedo missing a target and running past a convoy, could be catastrophic.

Barb did get a shot at a tanker, hit her, and did some damage, but not enough to keep her and two escorts from taking off toward a port on Formosa. There was no way to trail the wounded ship while submerged—it was too dangerous to chase on the surface in daylight. Still, maybe the vessel was in bad enough shape that the big load of fuel would take a long time to get to Luzon.

One kill. One hit with damage. And *Barb* was just getting started.

Suddenly, there were targets galore. *Barb* spotted smoke on the horizon just after noon on January 8. At least seven sources of smoke. A big convoy steaming south, likely to Takao on the south end of Formosa, a spot protected by a major Japanese naval presence. If they got too far past *Barb,* they would be into the relative safety of a subterranean minefield farther south. Fluckey told his crew they would line up on a good target and sink it from the west side. That would send the rest of the ships bolting in a more easterly direction, away from the shallow water along the China coast, right into the mitts of the other Loughlin's Loopers, *Queenfish* and *Picuda.*

The target *Barb* settled on was the *Anyo Maru,* a ten-thousand-ton munitions carrier. Unbeknownst to Fluckey, the ship also had kamikaze pilots, hundreds of troops, and vital military supplies on board. After chasing on the surface and allowing the other subs to catch up, *Barb* went under, put up the periscope, confirmed bearing and range, and quickly fired all six torpedoes from the forward tubes.

Three of them hit home with such a ferocious blast that men on the submarine feared it would take them down, too. Fluckey was so intent on setting up for his next shot that he failed to notice crewmembers sprawled all over the conning tower deck, and the thick haze of insulation and dust in the air. The boat had been knocked so far sideways by the explosions that everything had to be recalculated. They were shoved twenty feet below periscope depth and had to come back up to take a look. Men in the forward torpedo room were having a tough time reloading while stumbling around on cans of food that had spilled all over the deck in their compartment. They would later find a big section of deck grating had been ripped away from the superstructure by the force of the target's detonation.

All along, they could hear sounds of ships breaking up and something heavy hitting the seafloor. Rigged for depth charge and silent running, Fluckey most wanted to check on the whining of the high-speed propellors of the escort vessels now racing about on the surface, looking for their attacker. He also wanted to see for himself what kind of damage *Barb* had unleashed in that hellish blast.

He asked for a depth reading. Not promising. There was only about 160 feet of seawater between them and mud. But he went to periscope depth anyway.

Fluckey surveyed a gruesome scene through the 'scope lens. One ship's bow was jutting out of the water, her stern likely resting on the bottom. Escorts were trying to rescue the surprisingly few survivors. A large freighter, afire, was attempting to stagger away. A third freighter was simply no longer there. As Fluckey later wrote, "There is nothing left but an enormous smoke cloud and flat flotsam; no lifeboats, nothing alive, nothing."

He could also see—and sonar confirmed it—the escorts were heading away from them, maybe confused by the violence of the explosions. They did not know the direction from which the torpedoes had come. Not from their shallow side, they must have assumed. No submarine would be operating between them and the twenty-mile stretch of shallow water to the coast.

Unorthodox methods: When they worked, they worked well.

8 JAN.

> 1747 *Can feel aggressiveness surging through my veins since the escorts are more scared than we are. Commenced reload forward. Destroyer suddenly turned towards and shifted to short scale.*

> 1748 *Maximum relative movement between destroyer and BARB. Nice spot for a down the throat shot but no torpedoes forward.*

> 1749 *Aggressiveness evaporated.*

Oddly, all the other ships in the convoy had stopped, clearly not sure where to run. They were out of the range of the submarine's torpedoes. Then one of the destroyers turned and headed straight for *Barb*'s periscope.

Another of Fluckey's keys to success: not taking unnecessary chances. Live to fight another day.

"Go to 140 feet. All ahead flank! Right full rudder!"

A quick, fast turn might hopefully leave enough cavitation—basically noisy bubbles—and swirling water to confuse the destroyer's sonar. It worked. The escort zoomed on past and never dropped a single ash can.

Just after seven p.m., *Queenfish* sent word she was ready to take advantage of the falling darkness with an attack. Time was of the essence. The massive minefield was just south of them. And the China coast was less than twenty miles to the west. The convoy would certainly take advantage of either or both to ride out the night somewhere relatively safe, unreachable by the submarines.

Eugene Fluckey wanted to try something else. Wolfpacks typically tried to pick off lead ships in a convoy, which slowed those coming from behind, making them better targets. Fluckey wanted to do the unexpected and come up from behind, sinking the last ship in line. Then the next. And so on.

Like most of the CO's untraditional tactics, it worked like a charm. With the other two submarines attacking from the flanks, and with the ships in the convoy concentrating on evading them, *Barb* ran on the surface, right up to point-blank firing distance. Up ahead of them, they could see the results of *Picuda*'s torpedoes, triggering a fiery explosion on the lead ship in the convoy. And also see one of the destroyers running toward *Picuda*. But all that light and noise distracted the convoy. *Barb* slipped up on their starboard quarter from the rear.

Three of the submarine's fish took out two ships. Three more caused such a massive explosion on a tanker that the men on the sub's bridge were almost blown overboard. Fluckey would colorfully describe the blast in the boat's patrol log entry on January 8 at 2305: "Three hits timed and observed followed by a stupendous, earthshaking eruption. This far surpassed Hollywood and was one of the biggest explosions of the war. The rarefaction following the first pressure wave was breathtaking. A high vacuum resulted in the boat. Personnel in the control room said they felt as if they were being sucked up the hatch. Personnel in the Conning Tower, wearing shortened shirts not tucked in at the belt, had their shirts pulled up over their heads. On the bridge as the air was wrenched from my lungs, somehow it formed the words 'all ahead flank'. The target now resembled a gigantic phosphorus bomb . . . the volcanic spectacle was awe inspiring. Shrapnel flew all around us, splashing on the water in a splattering pattern as far as 4,000 yards ahead of us. Topside we alternately ducked and gawked. The horizon was lighted bright as day."

Amazingly, the escorts that had been running near the tanker were no longer there. Fluckey and his officers on the bridge were certain they had been sunk, caught up in the massive blast. The CO considered claiming them as kills. But he wrote in the log, "I figure that 4 ships sunk, one probably sunk and one damaged is about all the traffic will bear for a twelve torpedo expenditure." Only one ship in the convoy remained afloat, undamaged. Though Fluckey was willing to risk entering the minefield and go after it, *Queenfish* saved them the trouble. Elliott Loughlin and his guys made certain that ship would never reach the Philippines, either.

Queenfish staged another attack on a lone tanker the next day but missed with all eight torpedoes she fired. That was all she had left. Loughlin pointed his boat back toward Midway, leaving the active hunting grounds to *Picuda* and *Barb*.

After retiring to his stateroom, Gene Fluckey could not find sleep. He played over and over in his mind the furious action of the last five or six hours. What could he have done better? But something else kept running through his head, too. During one of the attacks, he had kept up an almost continuous description of what he was seeing through the 'scope, offering wry commentary. At one point, someone else in the conning tower had mumbled, "What does it take to make him afraid?"

Could it be he was becoming too cavalier? Why did fear not rule him as it had so many of the skippers who had come into the war with plenty of experience and expertise with submarines? Could such an attitude lead to a mistake that could cost him and all these fine young men their lives?

Fluckey decided that he indeed did feel fear, but more so in situations over which he had no control. Specifically, his wife and daughter, half a planet away. On *Barb*, he was in control, could take charge and do something about whatever was happening, and resist the temptation to do something too foolhardy.

He finally fell asleep, thinking of his family, and vowing to work even harder to bring this war to a conclusion as quickly as he could.

Then there was little he could do. Nothing for two full weeks. As if someone had thrown a switch, there were no more targets convoying through the previously congested Formosa Strait. Fluckey suspected the Japanese had found an alternate route. But the only one he could imagine was much too shallow for a ship of any size to be able to swim through.

Then he heard reports relayed from Chinese coast watchers that the coastline route Fluckey was thinking about had, indeed, been recently dredged. Even a massive battleship had reportedly made the transit. The targets they sought were now winding their way through newly deepened water snug up to the China coast and partially behind islands and rocky shoals that were strung offshore like a necklace. Protected, too, by lethal minefields.

The crew of *Barb* were elated when their skipper told them they had a promising new hunting area. Fluckey had already noted they were losing their edge, their spirit, the result of boredom and lack of action from mostly dodging airplanes and not shooting at anything. Now they were thrilled to get back to it.

Word came that a large convoy was headed their way and Fluckey was certain it would be taking the new, "safe" route. He took *Barb* to within fifteen miles of the coast, hiding in broad daylight among a fleet of Chinese fishermen in their junks. He had already established that the Chinese had no love for the Japanese. They would not report the presence of an American submarine in their midst. With the shape of her older sail, *Barb* on the surface blended nicely with the junks.

It was a good thing they mingled in so well. There was little water beneath the sub's keel should they need to hide.

Before long, the convoy report was confirmed when smoke on the horizon suggested at least six large vessels were steaming south along the new route. At one point, the lookouts could see the tops of masts, confirming six big vessels. *Barb* pulled away and, farther out at sea, made a quick run on the surface to an ambush point at about where the train of enemy vessels would pass just after dark, assuming they maintained their current course and speed. The submarine settled in between two deserted islands and did her best impression of a rock. The sonar of the escorts would not even notice them until the shooting started. *Barb* would pick them off as they passed, like tin targets in a carnival booth.

They waited. And waited. Nothing.

Picuda was farther south to take on elements of the convoy that made it past *Barb*. Fluckey checked with his old Annapolis classmate, Ty Shepard, *Picuda*'s CO. He confirmed no convoy had passed him. The only possibility was that the ships had already stopped in some unknown harbor or reasonably safe anchorage to ride out the night.

So, Fluckey declared, they would just enter the newly scraped-out channel and work northward, looking for all those desirable targets. They relied on the fishing junks to indicate waters where there were likely no mines floating. As they accelerated out of the hiding place between the two islands, Fluckey turned to his XO, Jim Webster, and said, "Let's gallop!" Webster grinned and responded, "The galloping ghost of the China coast!"

Fluckey liked that nickname. "The Galloping Ghost of the China Coast" had a nice ring to it. Plus, it did not apply only to the CO. The "ghost" was *Barb* and her entire crew.

As they steamed north, Fluckey knew that what he was about to do simply was not done: attack an anchored convoy in tight, rock-bound quarters and dangerously shallow water, ply waters that were heavily mined, rely on unreliable charts, and do it with only twelve torpedoes left, four in the tubes up front, eight in the stern tubes and on the skids back there, ready to load. Then attempt to escape on a course that offered no option for diving and hiding.

If *Barb* attacked and then needed to bug out, she would have to run on the surface for at least ten miles to find enough water to submerge.

23 JAN. (1945)

> **0300** *SHIP CONTACT #5B. Rounded INCOG*
> *ISLANDS and had radar contact on a very large*
> *group of anchored ships in the lower reaches of*
> *NAMKWAN HARBOR. Slowed to take stock of*
> *the situation. Fully realize our critical position and*
> *the dangers involved.*

Later, after it was all over, Fluckey would bullet-point in an addendum to the patrol report the "critical positions" and those "dangers" he chose to set aside and proceed with the attack. Those would include:

a. Unknown mines, how many and where, in the area. The positioning of the junks and guesswork would be the only way to know exactly where he could take his submarine.

b. Intercepted radar confirmed there were at least three destroyers, one northeast of the other ships, one to the east, the direction from which a submarine attack would most likely come, and a third escort north of the convoy's anchorage in what passed for a little harbor. The third one was seemingly more concerned with keeping himself off the rocks than with somebody shooting at the ships he was shielding.

c. The wind and currents of the waning tide would work against them should they follow usual practice and fire their last volley from the stern tubes to make it easier to flee. That might hurt their aim or prevent them from using those fish at all.

d. Fluckey was considering attacking from the southeast, through a large area marked on the charts as "UNEX-PLORED." There were rocks there that would prevent escorts from being enthusiastic about pursuing the sub. It would also allow *Barb* to escape through a flock of fishing junks, which would also present a problem for the destroyers.

The CO expected countermeasures from the enemy would be "searchlights, gunfire, and hot pursuit." *Barb* would have to respond with torpedoes from the stern tubes, her deck guns, and, if it came to it, rifles and handguns, as they ran as quickly as they could to deep water. Or, at least, less shallow water, where they could get under enough so their shears did not stick out of the sea and raise a rooster tail. One positive observation: There would be no depth charges, since there was simply not enough water in this little basin.

f. "Inasmuch as our attack position will be 6 miles inside the 10 fathom curve and 19 miles inside the 20 fathom curve, we will require an hour's run before being forced down. Consequently our attack must be a complete surprise and the force of our attack must be sufficient to completely throw the enemy off balance . . . a speedy, darting, knife thrust attack will increase the probability of success."

Doing the unexpected. That was the only way *Barb* would be able to pull off one of the most daring submarine assaults in history, and hope to live to tell about it.

Fluckey was optimistic, though. He wrote, "Figure the odds are 10 to 1 in our favor. Man battle stations."

That was at 0320. Daylight would arrive just before 0600. They had to move soon.

There was a quick debate about whether to issue life vests to the crew in case they had to abandon ship. Fluckey settled the question. He nixed the idea.

"The atmosphere in the boat is electric," he later wrote. "The men are more tense than I have ever seen them . . . the control room is so quiet the proverbial pin would have sounded like a depth charge. Discarded the idea of life jackets as definitely alarmist, with so many hearts doing flip flops."

As they paused and made final preparations for the bold, risky attack, putting a final charge on the battery, the captain got on the boat's announce system. He told the crew, "Shipmates, we've got this convoy bottled up along the coast. We're going to find them and knock the socks off them. When we attack we'll strike and strike hard with eight torpedoes. We'll overwhelm him, topple him, keep him off balance until we've skidded out of the harbor. This surprise will be *Barb*'s greatest night, a night to remember. If you have any questions, I'm coming through the boat now."

Though their CO only made the announcement once, practically every sailor and officer aboard could recite that speech word for word for years to come.

Fluckey started in the forward torpedo room, telling the torpedomen to put their fish in the top and middle tubes and set them to run no deeper than six feet. They would likely have less than thirty feet of water beneath them and he did not want any of the weapons to get lost in the silt on the bottom.

As he passed the galley, he asked one of the cooks if he was glad he had come along for another run aboard *Barb* and if he was ready to sign up for the next patrol. "I'll tell you tomorrow" was the cook's sardonic reply.

Nobody had questions. All of them gave their skipper a thumbs-up or flashed a *V* sign. Fluckey sensed they were ready. He knew they would do well.

He had already contacted *Picuda*, which was less than an hour away, briefly describing what he was about to do and offering to wait for Shepard and his crew if they wanted to join in the party. The reply was quick and telling: "Drop dead!"

Visibility grew worse. Only radar kept them from hitting rocks or junks. Then, as they drew near the assemblage of targets, they saw one of the frigate escorts patrolling around the small island named Incog. Fluckey would wait until the escort was on the far side of the island, unable to see them. They would skirt the rocky bit of land at flank speed, remaining undetected. Then set up, shoot, and shove off.

When they got to their firing point, Fluckey, on the bridge, could not believe his eyes. Radar returns showed there were as many as thirty ships, lined up three deep, and a few more anchored closer to shore, a line of ships that stretched nearly two miles. Almost as if they were hulks arrayed for target practice.

"This, frankly, must be the most beautiful target of the war," the skipper logged. "Even an erratic torpedo can't miss."

What they had stumbled upon was, in reality, several separate convoys putting into Namkwan to assure they would be safe in the dark this night. Safe they were not. Not any longer. Fluckey and his crew were quickly selecting primary targets, first for the bow torpedoes and then for when they hastily spun around and fired from the stern tubes. It was, according to the CO, like a kid in a candy store, carefully selecting his favorites.

The first four torpedoes from the bow whooshed away at 0402. It took three minutes to turn the sub around, get information to the torpedo data computer, and fire four more from the stern tubes. Fluckey was worried that more than one torpedo would hit a ship. That would be a waste. They had a spread pattern set to prevent that, but the targets were simply so close together, overlapping each other.

Before any of the torpedoes had time to hit a target, *Barb* was already ramping up to flank speed, headed east, toward the Formosa Strait and enough water to hide. No time, certainly, to reload the stern tubes with their last four torpedoes. Those might serve a purpose anyway if the escort ships spotted the sub and gave chase.

Captain Fluckey was on the bridge when the first torpedo struck home. Over the next three and a half minutes, he saw all eight hit and explode. But there were so many hellish detonations and eruptions of fire and debris that it was difficult to count victims. He was certain four were sinking and innumerable more were likely sinking or severely damaged. A couple of especially vicious blasts indicated ammunition or bombs. So massive that one or two had to be munitions ships. No way, though, to tell how many convoy mates went down with them.

The chaos set off by the Galloping Ghost was astonishing to behold.

Even better, searchlights that sprang up were searching the skies overhead. Air search radar went online, sweeping for bombers. The Japanese assumed this massive attack had to have come from the sky. A submarine in this shallow pool was not even a consideration. Any other kind of Allied warship capable of unleashing so much hell would have painted giant pips on the escorts' radar screens before firing.

Fluckey wrote, "The BARB is now high-balling it for the 20 fathom curve at 21.6 knots, broken field running through the Junk fleet . . . expect to see a Junk piled up on the bow any second."

Then came word from radar that one of the escorts had turned and appeared to be coming at *Barb*—coming fast! Somebody had finally realized it was a submarine.

Fluckey confirmed that the men in the aft torpedo room had reloaded, and gun crews were assembled in the control room, ready to go topside. He told the engine room to deliver every knot of speed the four big diesel engines could muster.

"Range to the escort?" Fluckey requested.

"Thirty-six hundred yards and closing."

Fluckey thought their pursuer looked to be a frigate. She

would not try to shoot the submarine until closing at least to within two thousand yards.

The engine room called up to the bridge to tell the skipper that the bearings were getting red-hot. Fluckey told them to let the bearings melt. Governors on the engines, designed to protect them if they were pushed too hard, were on the verge of locking down, cutting off the engines entirely. Fluckey told the men to override the governors. They could not afford to have the frigate get close enough to start shooting.

The frigate was at 3,200 yards, still closing, but not as quickly. Barb was making 23.5 knots. "A new world's record for a submarine," one of the officers declared with no hint of a smile.

Then Fluckey had an idea. He would steer a course near an area of rocks. If the frigate got close enough to flip on his lights in preparation for opening fire, *Barb* would send his way two of the torpedoes from the stern tubes. Even if they missed, there was a chance the escort would spin around for a broadside salvo, employing more of their guns than was possible if the bow was pointed at the sub—and there was a good chance he would run aground on the many rocks in the area.

It was a good plan, deflected by the presence of a sea full of fishing junks. Fluckey steered *Barb* near the bigger rocks and a small island, then began running a dizzying course through the little boats. Just then, the frigate opened fire, not at the submarine but at the poor fishermen. Fluckey snorted. The inferior radar the Japanese were using had led them to mistake the junks for their original target. Their radar was so bad, it could not tell the difference between a submarine and a fleet of fishing boats.

The turn of events was bad for the fishermen, but it was

enough confusion to allow *Barb* to hurry on. The frigate never turned on his searchlights, giving the sub a point of aim for the loaded torpedoes. Just as well. *Barb* had done a decent night's worth of work already.

0445 *Sent contact report to PICUDA.*

0511 *The Galloping Ghost of the China Coast crosses the 20 fathom curve with a sigh. Never realized how much water that was before. However, life begins at 40 (fathoms). Kept going.*

0550 *Dawn. Assume the Japs will expect us to submerge, so will stay on the surface.*

Why change tactics now? They unstrapped the governors and slowed to seventeen knots to allow things to cool down. No one was chasing the *Barb* any longer, so why not stay on the surface and put maximum distance between them and the scene of all that mischief? It also gave Fluckey an opportunity to radio a report to the wolfpack commander, Ty Shepard, on *Picuda*. Fluckey could not resist a dig at his old friend. He invited Shepard to join him for another night's hunting among the tiny bays, treacherous rocks, mined harbors, and fog-shrouded islands of the China coast. Shepard tersely replied once again, "Drop dead."

An airplane eventually appeared, just after 6:30 a.m., forcing them under. That gave them yet another opportunity to splice the main brace in celebration. Fluckey was also informed he had just spent twenty-four hours bouncing up and down between the bridge and the conning tower. Someone else casually mentioned that the skipper would absolutely receive the Medal of Honor for what he had just done. Fluckey bristled a bit. He was no seeker of medals, he said. His goal was never to earn medals. It was to inflict maximum damage on the enemy and end the war.

When the sub surfaced again, a bit past noon, Fluckey was "retiring to east. Requested China Air Force obtain information as to damage inflicted in harbor." Curiosity was killing the captain. "Eight hits, no errors," he told the crew. He could not wait to see what credit *Barb* would receive.

They continued to patrol, looking for a worthy recipient of their last four torpedoes. The only thing they could find was no comparison to the last collection: a three-ship convoy. Rain was coming down in torrents and the seas were exceedingly rough. All four torpedoes missed. The lucky targets never even knew they were being shot at.

Barb arrived back at Midway on February 9, then steamed on to Pearl Harbor, docking there on February 15. Along the way, Fluckey learned that there would be no public mention or recognition yet for *Barb*'s remarkable feat in Namkwan. The whole glorious episode was to be kept under wraps to avoid endangering the other boats operating there. This despite the fact that Chinese newspapers had already reported extensively on the whole conflagration.

Fluckey also emphasized that he did not want his crew to go around bragging about their accomplishments, spectacular as they were. Not even when the news eventually came out. Shipping was becoming hard to find. Targets were few and far between for subs. Boats were coming back from patrol with what the skippers called "an empty bag." No point in starting fistfights ignited by resentment and jealousy. Besides, their fine submarine would now be going on to Mare Island, California, for a much-needed overhaul. And that meant shore leave for her crew. The captain was hoping to get going to the West Coast on the eighteenth. However, he was informed that he had an audience with Admiral Nimitz's deputy and other admirals to explain exactly how he and his boat had done what they had there on the China coast. They would have to delay departure for California by one day.

The meeting with the admirals led to a very pointed set of questions from those assembled. The dour-faced group seemed wary about how much time Fluckey kept his submarine on the surface. They also rather solemnly inquired about the skipper's decision to not have his men wear life jackets during the assault at Namkwan.

When Fluckey was dismissed from the meeting, he was convinced that the admirals did not understand or appreciate his unconventional ideas on running a submarine. How well it worked did not appear to matter.

Not for the first time, Gene Fluckey felt he might be in trouble.

Admiral "Babe" Brown, deputy commander and another one of Uncle Charlie's right-hand men, was Lockwood's proxy for Fluckey's meeting and debriefing. He asked Gene to wait outside for him. Ten minutes later, Brown stepped out of the conference room, a somber look on his face.

"Gene," he said. "Do you know what you've just done?"

"Not really. They were so quiet and had so few questions."

"Skipper, they were not quiet. They were stunned. Admiral Nimitz had a secondary purpose for this meeting. You are going to receive the Medal of Honor. Based on this debrief, it is now approved."

For once, Eugene Fluckey was speechless. For all his talk about not going to battle hoping to win medals, he was honored now to join a very special group. Honored, that is, so long as it was presented as an award to and honor for all the officers and men of USS *Barb*.

The citation for Fluckey's Medal of Honor would read, in part:

"For conspicuous gallantry and intrepidity at the risk of his life above and beyond the call of duty as Commanding Officer of the U.S.S. Barb during her Eleventh War Patrol along the east coast of China from 19 December 1944, to 15 February 1945. After sinking a large enemy ammunition ship and damaging additional tonnage during a running two-hour night battle on 8 January, Commander Fluckey, in an exceptional feat of brilliant deduction and bold tracking on 23 January, located a concentration of more than 30 enemy ships in the lower reaches of Nankuan Chiang (Namkwan Harbor). Fully aware that a safe retirement would necessitate an hour's run at full speed through the uncharted, mined, and rock-obstructed waters, he bravely ordered, 'Battle Station—Torpedoes!' In a daring penetration of the heavy enemy screen, and riding in five fathoms of water, he launched the Barb's last forward torpedoes at 3,000-yard range. Quickly bringing the ship's stern tubes to bear, he turned loose four more torpedoes into the enemy, obtaining eight direct hits on six of the main targets to explode a large ammunition ship and cause inestimable damage by the resultant flying shells and other pyrotechnics. Clearing the treacherous area at high speed, he brought the Barb through to safety . . . to complete a record of heroic combat achievement, reflecting the highest credit upon Commander Fluckey, his gallant officers and men, and the United States Naval Service.

It would be a month later before Fluckey learned *Barb's* accepted eleventh-patrol tally. That came after staffers sifted through the patrol report, looked at data from other sources, and came up with a total. She would be credited with sinking seven ships and get partial credit for three more, shared with *Picuda* and *Queenfish*. That would be sixty thousand tons of Japanese shipping. She would also be credited with damaging four other vessels for 26,500 tons.

In his final endorsement to Fluckey's patrol report, COM-SUBPAC Chief of Staff Merrill Comstock termed the patrol a "history-making fighting performance." The commander of Submarine Squadron Four, W. V. O'Regan, called it "one of the most outstanding patrols of the war." Pacific submarine force commander Admiral Charles Lockwood was his typical effusive self when he praised *Barb's* eleventh run, saying, "The BARB, continuing her illustrious record, turned in a performance during this patrol which is probably an all-time record."*

Lockwood's highest praise likely came, though, when he

---

* It was, at the time, but JANAC accounting would reduce the total number of ships sunk by the submarine by more than half. Even so, the boat's eleventh run was one of the top patrols of World War II—and, without question, one of its most spectacular.

added, "This patrol should be studied in detail by submarine personnel."

And it would be. Not only by submarine personnel, but by the Navy, other branches of the service, naval historians, and many others.

As Gene Fluckey enjoyed weeks away from the war during the California refit, and precious time with Marjorie and Barbara, he contemplated the even more interesting tactics he hoped to experiment with on the twelfth run. Assuming he would get the patrol area he was lobbying for, and assuming Uncle Charlie kept his promise and let him take *Barb* out there one more time.

Fluckey had another thought when he read Lockwood's suggestion that the patrol report be studied by other personnel.

He would have loved to see the face of one particular person as he perused the report of *Barb*'s most recent run—someone he had in mind as the captain wrote the descriptions of the various attacks in the submarine's log and handed them to his yeoman to type up.

Gene wished he could see the face of Franklin Roosevelt as the president continued to follow the daring exploits of USS *Barb* and her dynamic captain and crew.

CHAPTER SEVENTEEN

"THE IDEAL SUBMARINE BOMBARDMENT"

It certainly did not feel like the first day of July, a week and a half into summer. It was cold and foggy. Ice floated in the sea all around the surfaced USS *Barb* as she once again transited the waters of the Sea of Okhotsk north of the Japanese Home Island of Hokkaido, within spitting distance of Sakhalin Island and Japanese-held territory. A part of the Empire of Japan, at least for now. Japan and Russia had disputed who owned this godforsaken, snow-bedecked, volcano-smoke-belching land for centuries. Trees, fish, seals, and frozen dirt filled with valuable metals and ore. Those natural resources were the attraction. Certainly not the weather.

Even so, doing something positive, even in frigid weather, would hopefully boost the mood of the *Barb* crew, and the mood of her commanding officer as well. What had begun as a stellar twelfth patrol for one of the US Navy's most praised submarines had turned decidedly sour over the last few days. They had stalked a sizable Japanese convoy down the east coast of Sakhalin and into Patience Bay, waiting for the ships to commit to a direction of travel once they steamed out of the shallows and into deep, open water. *Barb* had them dead to rights—even though they were being shielded by one of the Imperial Japanese Navy's newest and deadliest antisub destroyers.

But after taking a pounding from both the escort and buzzing aircraft, and by the time *Barb* had wasted a dozen torpedoes that simply did not go where they were supposed to, the sub had been forced to slink away and allow all those targets to steam off unharmed.

So close. So close to a haul that might possibly have rivaled the amazing one they had enjoyed off the China coast on their previous run—a haul that came after considerable disappointment early in the run, the men reminded each other: the assault on the massive collection of ships in Namkwan Harbor.

Gene Fluckey knew how men thought. Especially submarine sailors. He recognized that the debacle in Patience Bay—though not at all their fault—had them feeling down and out. They had lost that edge he knew they would need before Fluckey's final run as CO of *Barb* was completed. That was why he had them out there in the icy fog, preparing to do the next thing nobody in submarines had ever done.

1 JULY, 1945

Surface patrolling . . . our first fog in the area.

1330 *Tested out both rubber boats with four, 200 lbs. plus, Officers in view of anticipated future operations.*

2030 *Set course for KAIHYO TO for morning bombardment. This island contains a large government operated seal rookery on the eastern side. Buildings and warehouses are located on the western side. We plan to land and take it. A prisoner will be valuable to check routing and frequency of KURILE Convoys.*

Nowhere in the curricula for those attending the Navy's submarine school in New London, Connecticut, was there any mention of training for such an operation. But Eugene Fluckey had vowed that, if he was only granted one more wartime patrol as CO on a submarine, he would show the Navy that the plunging boats were good for far more than shooting torpedoes, hoping for a hit as the boat ran away to hide.

He had already used his best sales pitch just to convince Admiral Lockwood to allow him a fifth patrol at the helm of *Barb*. Then he had to sell and sell hard when he and his sub were initially assigned lifeguard duty off Midway because tradition forbade Medal of Honor recipients from being sent directly back into combat. And finally, he had cashed in every chip he had in order to be allowed to take aboard a cache of experimental rockets. That was so he could prove just how effective a rocket launch platform submarines could be. They were well on their way to demonstrating that point after inflicting significant damage on facilities at the port of Shari, on Japanese soil on Hokkaido.

Now here they were, floating around in rubber boats among ice cubes, hoping to jump-start this run and salvage a spectacular war patrol. With no other convoys showing up, now appeared to be an opportune time to prove another concept.

When the captain shared his plan for rowing ashore and capturing Kaihyo Island, he asked for volunteers. Every sailor aboard raised his hand. There was only room for four or five men in each of the recently tested inflatable boats. The captain settled on a total of eight volunteers, but they had to be the correct eight.

Fluckey had final say but listened to input from his officers and chief petty officers. He picked a photographer to capture the action, a radioman who would know what communications equipment to spend time and effort destroying, a signalman, a gunner's mate, a machinist's mate who would best know how to put machinery out of service, and three men who could hold their own in a street fight. Training began immediately, revealing the plan, and training each man on how to use the boat's automatic weapons, the "tommy guns."

The plan was to attack late the night of July 1, but the fog only grew thicker. Fluckey wanted to be able to see it all, from initial bombardment to the boats returning with a prisoner. Excitement among the crew waned only slightly. They knew the mission would happen. Fluckey had decreed it! The only thing likely to stop the assault would be if they spotted or received word of a convoy coming their way, but there was still nothing happening in that department.

They took one more look at the island in predawn light the next morning. Final plans were made. They would approach from the west. The barrage would begin with *Barb* a thousand yards offshore, using the forty-millimeter gun to see if there would be return fire. Then they would open up with the five-inch gun "for destruction." The two twenty-millimeter guns would take aim at any small-arms fire. If the deck gunners did their job, the assault party should encounter only minimal resistance.

As *Barb* rounded the southern tip of the little island, they noticed something that was not there when Fluckey and his crew passed by the previous year, on their eighth patrol.

> 0625 *Headed in for bombardment. Was a bit surprised to find 20 or more large barracks, warehouses and buildings on the western side. Looks like business has expanded beyond our expectations . . .*

> 0638 *Commenced continuous keying of fathometer.*

> 0641 *Manned battle stations—gun.*

XO Jim Webster gave his skipper a questioning look as those new buildings came into view.

"The more the merrier," Fluckey responded. "All ahead full!"

The need for seal oil and sealskins had increased, yet the Japanese had overhunted the area. That required more people to go out and bring back the animals. The IJN had also realized the strategic value of the small island and presently had a group of radar technicians doing a major installation there. With this increased importance, a company of soldiers was now stationed on Kaihyo to protect the uptick in activity.

As *Barb* settled in about a thousand yards off the beach, constantly checking to see how much water they had beneath them—which, at that spot, was only seven fathoms—they could see men madly running about onshore. Some wore navy uniforms. Others were clearly Japanese Army.

Barb had been spotted and the men on the island realized she was not a friendly vessel.

The first shot from the submarine's forty-millimeter deck gun went out at 6:51 a.m. Return fire was almost simultaneous. Most of it was not reaching the sub, but they would have to put a stop to it before they could safely put men on boats into the water. The worst of it was from a fifty-caliber gun mounted in the open atop a cliff. It was quickly taken out with the forty-millimeter. Return fire ceased. Next, the sub's five-inch gun systematically aimed at each building in order, setting each of them on fire. The new radar station and the island's radio facility were wiped out. Other gunners concentrated on several sampans docked there, splintering them. Soon raging fires leapt from building to building, quickly consuming them. Thick black smoke boiled high into a clear morning sky. A photographer who was making this run on the *Barb*—one of the men who planned to soon be in a boat going ashore—described the scene perfectly, saying, "Through my movie camera it looks like Vesuvius erupting."

Barb was now seven hundred yards from shore and sitting in a mere six fathoms—thirty-six feet—of water. The deck gunners were having a field day. It was the first time for most of them to actually see the damage they were unleashing. The gun crew was made up of torpedomen and enginemen and electricians. They typically only heard the explosions they helped cause during a normal submarine attack.

Fluckey would later write, "Really a wonderful sight and the ideal submarine bombardment—huge fires burning, sections of buildings flying up into the air, Sampans destroyed, oil drums tumbled and split, a field piece overturned and a machine gun hanging loose, unattended. Too much praise cannot be given the gun crews."

The skipper was especially pleased with how frugal the gunners were with their limited ammunition. "Not a bullet or shell was wasted," he documented in the patrol log.

Next, according to plan, the submarine backed away and headed out about three miles, in water deep enough to dive. They did not know if a distress message might have made its way from the radio station before it was obliterated, though radiomen on *Barb* had detected no signals on the usual Japanese frequencies. If there had been an SOS, though, airplanes might appear at any minute.

When no aircraft or warships showed up, Fluckey eased the boat back toward the island at about 10:30 in the morning. As they did, they inflated the two rubber boats. They could now see that, if anything, the fires consuming the buildings had intensified. As they came to a stop, the trim tanks were flooded, lowering the bow and making it easier to get the boats and assault team into the water.

Fluckey had thought of everything. As he came down from the bridge to shake each man's hand, he gave one of them an

American flag to run up the pole on Kaihyo. It was not exactly Mount Suribachi on Iwo Jima, but it would be one more bit of captured territory for the USA. The skipper told the men that if anything happened to their rubber boats, he would "put the bow of *Barb* on the beach and haul you aboard."

The sub crept in closer, to about six hundred yards from where the sampans had been tied up. There were only fragments there now. At least ten pairs of binoculars scanned the island for any sign of human movement. Men hung in the shears, keeping an eye out, while gun crews stayed ready.

Just after eleven a.m., as they approached four hundred yards from shore and the launching point in bright sunshine, only moments before putting the two boats into the water, both the CO and officer of the deck noticed something ominous: four pillboxes. At least one of them was manned, ready to fire if anyone attempted to go ashore, or to fire on the submarine when the time was right.

Fluckey immediately sent the order to fire the forty-millimeter gun at the one that obviously held a gun crew and sported a radio antenna as well. There was quick return fire, machine guns and rifles. All *Barb*'s deck guns opened up. In moments, the primary pillbox had its front blown away and any other weapons fire was silenced.

Gene Fluckey closed his eyes and considered the situation for a long moment. He ordered the submarine to back away. A daylight landing was simply too risky.

As a confirmation of the correctness of his decision, when they were about four thousand yards out from the shoreline of what the crew had dubbed Little Iwo Jima, there was considerable machine-gun fire in their direction from the island. Fluckey termed it "a face-saving measure." The bullets fell way short, of course, but Fluckey did not want to think what might have happened had he put those boats and eight good men in the water and the enemy had opened up on them from the pillbox.

As they retreated, the captain picked up the microphone and addressed the crew on the boat's intercom system.

"Men, I realize that the rubber boats are not all that have been deflated, myself included. But I cannot praise the gun crews too much, nor the alertness of our lookouts, nor our volunteer assault force. Regretfully, there were too many military, too well dug in."

He went on to pronounce the effort as "the ideal submarine bombardment," reminding the crew that they had put an important enemy installation out of business. He offered "a hearty well done to all."

Besides, the captain soon had the boat headed in the direction of their next potential conquest. That was Shikuka, a major city resting on the northwestern shore of Patience Bay, a spot where many of the men on the submarine had been before—where on a foggy night they had come close to launching torpedoes at a couple of factory smokestacks far off the beach. A place to which he had vowed to return one day and counter that embarrassing episode.

He and some of his officers felt their training for the aborted assault on the little island would still be put to use before this run was completed. They certainly hoped so.

Fluckey did not know at the time just how his boat's attack on the island would be perceived by the enemy. It would have been perfect for his morale-building speech on the intercom had he been able to quote from later news accounts and the enemy's final report. But it was long after the end of World War II when the skipper learned that a story in the *Japanese Army News* had quoted the survivors of the attack on Kaihyo To. They reported that three enemy ships attacked their island, that a submarine later joined the assault, and that between six hundred and seven hundred bombs fell on them. The survivors were eventually rescued, and Little Iwo Jima was abandoned.

A Japanese naval officer who was on the island during *Barb*'s bombardment later compiled the final report on the incident.

In closing, the officer sadly noted, "Only the seals came back to the island as if nothing had happened."

CHAPTER EIGHTEEN

THE SUBMARINE THAT "SANK" A TRAIN

Fluckey and his crew were ready to use their rockets again. The industrial city of Shikuka was the perfect target on a perfect night, and a perfect opportunity to nullify an embarrassing event, too. Shikuka was the place where *Barb* had moved in through thick fog to attack the Japanese war fleet but, just before putting the submarine onto the beach, realized those "ships" so prominent on radar were factory smokestacks.

3 JULY 1945

> 0100 *Sighted range lights of SHIKUKA harbor. Heavy overcast and a light drizzle. Perfect for rocketeering. Set up rocket launcher and checked circuits.*

0210 *Manned battle stations—rockets. Loaded 12 rockets.*
Set rocket range at 5250 yards. Target to be center
of town with drift going into factories.

0239 *ROCKET ASSAULT #2 . . . put on polaroid*
goggles to watch the fun.

0240 *ROCKETS AWAY!!!*

But nothing happened. No rockets whooshing away to arc into the city. Just the quiet lapping of water against the hull of the submarine.

Members of the launch crew began frantically checking, trying to figure what had gone wrong. They found a loose connection, a wire likely broken when someone tripped over it in the dark. They quickly spliced it.

Seven minutes later, they tried again. This time, everything worked.

The rockets landed "with their usual thunder and explosions amongst a mass of buildings." There were no immediate fires, but lights blinked on and off, then stayed off. Radar was detected but it was sweeping skyward, looking for what defenders believed were the aircraft that had dropped bombs on their city.

Barb could not stick around to watch. They hurried back out into Patience Bay, as always looking for deeper water. They had been in a place too shallow to dive—less than twenty-five feet— when they shot their rockets into Shikuka.

Besides, Fluckey had another reason to hurry on. He fully expected that the enemy would rush a response to the northern part of the bay after what *Barb* had done there and at Kaihyo

To. They would assume it was a submarine wolfpack. But by that time, the Galloping Ghost would be way down at La Pérouse Strait wreaking havoc there.

Later in the day, they paused to sink a freighter northbound for Shikuka. *Barb* used one of the smaller Mark 27 acoustic-homing torpedoes. It worked far better than the larger Mark 28s had, sinking the ship before Fluckey could even get to the surface to take a look. They did manage to retrieve some updated sea charts from the vessel's pilothouse, which had been blown free. It still floated but was going down quickly. Fluckey noted that the charts were dated 1936. The charts the sub had been relying on were from 1894. More important, the newer charts clearly indicated where the minefields were strewn about in the waters of the region. Only later did Fluckey and his officers realize that this simple sinking of a freighter was another first for USS *Barb*: the first freighter sunk by a "cutie," an acoustic torpedo.

They continued to see—and almost accidentally shot torpedoes at—several Russian ships, including a destroyer. Allied vessels operating in the area were supposed to be kept up to date on the presence of Russian warships, but it was obvious that was not being done. On July 5, as *Barb* was stalking a pair of Japanese freighters, they were unintentionally blocked by Russian freighters emerging from the same harbor near the La Pérouse Strait. After a wait, Fluckey and his crew were able to shoot at and sink the larger of the Japanese ships, watching and filming through the periscope as it broke apart and sank. No thanks to Joseph Stalin, who still procrastinated about joining the war against Japan. That would not happen for another month, August 8, 1945, three months after the end of the war in Europe and two days after the first US atomic bomb fell on Hiroshima, and only one week before Japan officially surrendered.

Around midday on July 6, a smiling radioman brought his skipper a transcript of a broadcast picked up from Radio Tokyo. It told of an attack on the city of Shikuka a few nights before by "five enemy ships," all of which were still likely plying the waters of the Sea of Okhotsk.

Fluckey hooted. *Barb* had been mistaken for five ships!

That night, the submarine was part of yet another odd occurrence, something that had become typical for Gene Fluckey's graduation patrol. An hour before dark, they spotted a lugger—a two- or three-mast sailing ship—running along the coast. Since they had not seen anything else to shoot at that was not Russian, they stalked the vessel and, with darkness approaching, launched a surface gun attack as their quarry raced to get into a harbor. The sub fired several shells, but before *Barb* could hit the fleeing lugger, the sub was chased back out to deeper water by the sudden appearance of an aircraft.

As Fluckey watched through the 'scope, two cannons onshore opened up, lobbing shells seaward. No worries: *Barb* was well beyond where the ordnance was splashing into the sea. After dropping one bomb, the plane appeared to no longer know where the submarine was.

Then XO Jim Webster, who was watching from the other 'scope, realized something. The cannons were shooting not at *Barb* but at the lugger. The sub's few misses before turning away had obviously caused some panic ashore and they assumed the shelling came from the sailing vessel. As Webster watched, a shell hit home and the lugger sank almost immediately.

"Do we claim credit, Captain?" Webster asked.

"Absolutely!" Fluckey responded. "Whether we get it or not, that's another thing. But we claim credit."

That night, *Barb* received orders to steam almost five hundred miles southeast, out of the Sea of Okhotsk, through the Kunashiri Strait, past that telegraph station Fluckey still wanted to obliterate, and into the Pacific, all to do lifeguard duty off the east coast of Hokkaido. Because of the weather, the planned air strike was delayed. While there were no downed fliers to rescue, the sub was able to set up close enough to shore that they could direct other American bombers to some worthy targets.

Even so, Fluckey lamented the lost patrol time. This detour ultimately left them only about six days before they would need to head home. The skipper did some fuel calculations, had the cooks check the stores, then promptly sent a message to fleet headquarters to request a one-week extension. It was granted. Fluckey wished he could have seen Uncle Charlie's face when he heard Lucky Fluckey was refusing to come home from the patrol, one the admiral did not want him to make in the first place.

As they made the run back toward Patience Bay and La Pérouse Strait, Fluckey spent time in his stateroom considering maps and charts of a particular area on the eastern shore of the bay, a spot where they had paused one night to watch a busy rail line and discussed ways of damaging that particular means of transportation. They pondered ways to use the deck guns. The captured charts, though, confirmed the depth of the water would not allow them to get close enough. But if not their deck guns, how else?

Back in familiar waters, traffic was heavy: still quite a few

Russian ships. Cargo vessels, too, but usually escorted by frigates, and almost always in shallow or mined waters near the shoreline.

Then, about midday on July 18, a large freighter appeared, being shown the way by a frigate. Hardly a convoy but a couple of quite valid targets. As they scrambled to battle stations, torpedo, Fluckey collared Paul "Swish" Saunders, the chief of the boat (the top enlisted man aboard). The skipper shared with him that he was still considering taking out that rail line before they headed home. He asked his COB to spread the word, to see if any of the sailors had ideas for how it might be accomplished.

So, in the middle of a torpedo attack, Fluckey did something else few submarine skippers would have done: He asked members of his crew, and not just officers, for their thoughts on how to go about doing something.

"Everybody's ideas are welcomed," the skipper told Saunders as the "battle stations" gong sounded up and down the boat. "No matter how serious or silly."

Saunders knew exactly what his captain wanted. He was not surprised by the request, not even that it came during a surface attack on an enemy vessel.

He had been aboard *Barb* since her commissioning: a rarity— a plank owner now on his twelfth run on the same boat, and her COB for all of Fluckey's patrols. When new-captain Fluckey first asked Saunders to be his COB, the chief refused. Swish considered himself to be good friends with every man on *Barb*. No way he could be a tough disciplinarian, an SOB, which was typically expected of a COB. Fluckey explained that toughness was not necessarily what he was looking for. "Swish, I don't want a bastard. I want a leader," he told Saunders. "We don't drive men on the *Barb*. We lead them."

The chief accepted.

The attack went on, soon becoming a mixed blessing. The three-torpedo spread whooshed away, aimed for the cargo ship. Two of them missed everything. But the third, in a bit of good luck, slammed into the stern of the frigate, the point above which the warship carried a full load of depth charges. They detonated spectacularly. What was left of the vessel sank quickly, even as the freighter turned and ran.

"Serendipity!" Fluckey exclaimed.

Barb was out of conventional torpedoes. Only a few of the smaller acoustic ones remained. They had very short range compared to the regular fish. There was no hope of catching the freighter without going to the surface. In daylight, this close to numerous air bases, and after likely attracting significant interest by sinking the frigate, a chase would not be prudent.

Besides, the skipper was now pondering his next action. In a meeting in the wardroom, Swish Saunders brought in one of the sailors, an electrician's mate, who had worked for a railroad back home prior to the war. He had some very specific ideas on how to approach the captain's evolving plan. The idea now was to conduct a sabotage attack that would not only take out the busy railroad track but to also sink a train at the same time.

Everyone had settled on the idea of using one of the boat's scuttle charges. These devices contained torpex, a high explosive, and were designed to be set to blow up the submarine should there be a chance of it falling into enemy hands. Each "bomb" weighed fifty-five pounds and used a timer to set it off.

That was the problem. They could not count on a train arriving at a specific time at a spot where the scuttle charge had been placed. There was no way to remotely cause it to detonate, either. But the sailor—who just happened to be from West Virginia and was named Hatfield, a relative of those involved in the Hatfield and McCoy feud—had a potential solution.

As a kid, he and his buddies used freight trains to crack nuts. They placed walnuts beneath the rails and the weight of a passing train caused them to dip down enough to crack them. Hatfield suggested they disable the timer on the scuttle charge and use a microswitch beneath a rail to set off the blast and wreck the train.

Fluckey was ecstatic. It might just work!

But there were still problems to turn into solutions. First, of course, was who and how many men to send ashore in the two rubber rafts that never even got wet at Little Iwo Jima. Fluckey intended to be one of those men. Secondly, they would have to find a way to get to the tracks without being seen. Then they would need to bury the charge, which was fourteen inches by fourteen inches by sixteen inches, as well as the battery that powered the spark that made the thing blow up. Finally, they would have to place the switch so it was close enough to the rail that the weight of the train would close it—and set the switch without accidentally blowing themselves up in the process.

Oh, and do all that before someone spotted them. Or a train came rumbling down the track. Then get back into the boats and rendezvous with *Barb*. All this without risking the boat and her crew any more than necessary.

As the sun fell and *Barb* surfaced for a night of hunting, Gene Fluckey was uncharacteristically distracted, contemplating the attempt to blow up the train. He was convinced putting saboteur teams ashore and retrieving them after they had done their mischief was another valuable role for submarines. He could prove it, right here on the shore of Karafuto. So far as he knew, there had not been any Allied saboteur team sent ashore on any of the Japanese Home Islands yet, not in almost four years of war. Not by any means of insertion. He and his guys were about to be the first.

Fluckey, the design engineer, was also concerned about one small but significant point: just how far did a railway rail sag beneath a train whose weight they did not know? Enough to close the contacts on a microswitch? Was all the danger—a significant risk—worth it if they were not sure the sag would crack the walnut? After factoring in all the data he could find or estimate, he decided the rail would absolutely move downward by seven-tenths of an inch.

Maybe for the first time, the aggressive skipper was glad there were no worthy targets that night. Then, the next day, he remained in his stateroom, still doing calculations, looking over charts for the best route to creep near the shore, and choosing the men in the rubber boats.

Fluckey had heard rumblings that some of the men felt favoritism had been shown in the selection of the assault team for Kaihyo To. He vowed to be able to justify each choice for this mission. "I needed the strong, the smart, and the dependable, as well as widespread representation from the various ratings."

Everyone, from sailor to officer, would be considered for what he could offer to help assure success. He would give preference to unmarried men, pull equally from all departments on the boat, and at least half the team would have to have been Boy Scouts. They would have better survival skills in case they could not get back to the boat. In that case, and if they were not caught by the enemy, they would have to hike over rugged terrain to the northern reaches of Sakhalin Island, the part still held by Russia.

Obviously, Billy Hatfield, the electrician and former railroad worker, would be on the team. He would be the only married man among the group. Lieutenant Bill Walker would be the leader. Fluckey considered him the biggest and strongest man in his wardroom. He would be in one boat. COB Swish Saunders was a fine gunner and an obvious choice for second in command and leader of the second boat crew. For various equally good reasons, the rest of the party would include Ed Klinglesmith, John Markuson, Lawrence Newland, Neal Sever, and Jim Richard.

When Fluckey called in his executive officer to get his opinion of the list, the skipper also shared his intention to leave *Barb* in his XO's charge and be the ninth member of the shore party. Webster was aghast. He threatened to personally send a message to every one of Fluckey's bosses, telling them what his captain was proposing. He convinced his boss to give up the idea.

Everyone agreed with Fluckey's choices. Those picked were enthusiastic. Fluckey later maintained that if they had had twenty rubber boats, the whole crew would have gone ashore. Training began immediately. Equipment was chosen. Fluckey determined that Hatfield would be the one who would set the switch beneath the rail. The other five men—two would remain on the beach guarding the boats—would be at least twenty feet away, hunkered down, so if something went wrong, if the switch somehow got accidentally closed as it was being positioned, none of them would be hurt.

They decided to use birdcalls to communicate with one another while ashore, including the whistles of the quail and the whippoorwill. Then someone mentioned to Fluckey that there was a chance the Japanese would hear those calls and realize they were those of American birds, not native to these parts. Fluckey simply shook his head and told them they would rely on the Japanese not knowing their birdcalls any better than the average American did.

They had no pick or shovel, tools essential to dig a hole in the hard ground beneath the railroad track. These were not implements typically carried on a submarine. The engineers ripped up metal deck plating, used a cutting torch to shape them, and welded them to metal pipes for handles. Each man would wear a life jacket and carry a red-bulbed flashlight, along with watches, knives, D rations, a cigarette lighter, and a pistol. In the two boats, there would be carbines, tommy guns, hand grenades, a signal gun, a Very pistol (a flare gun), binoculars, and line. And, of course, a Mark 108 fifty-five-pound explosive device with associated electrical equipment. There was one last-minute addition. They secured some meat and liver from the galley just in case they encountered dogs on the way to the track.

July 19 presented a clear sky and a full, brilliantly bright moon. No sabotage that night. But they did creep in close enough to consider the topography and watch a long train go past. They selected the best place to put the submarine and the ideal landing position for the two rubber boats. There was a relatively level grassy area beyond the beach, then a highway, and beyond that, all the way to the railroad, was only scrubland. In darkness, it should be an easy transit for men on foot. Even while carrying a bomb.

But lack of darkness was a problem. They needed cloud cover to mask that moon.

20 JULY, 1945

1200 *A close study of the Japanese Charts of KARAFUTO recovered from the sinking of the coastal AK has revealed more accurate sounding information than our own charts. Selected a more suitable position for the sabotage.*

1517 *Dived and closed coast for observation.*

1947 *Sighted regular train. Previous observations have given us their timetables now. Selected optimum position for landing while we coasted with 2 fathoms beneath the keel. Sandy beach, no houses within 700 yards of spot and submarine could approach to 1000 yards from beach without grounding. Our plans have been laid for three long weeks, every detail checked, the waterproof firing system made up—now, all we*

> *await is 4 hours of darkness with the moon covered and a calm sea.*
>
> 2132 *Surfaced. Sea calm, but we are fouled up by a perfect lovers' night, a bright moon. Cloudless.*

The hours dragged. *Barb* continued to watch for something at which they might aim their few remaining small torpedoes. All the while, they tried not to think about the delayed sabotage mission. Fluckey knew the lack of activity, the diminishing edge each man had, and the disappointment after such a high state of involvement could seriously threaten the success of the sabotage mission, even the rest of the patrol. At some point, if the moon kept shining and as enthusiasm and diesel fuel ran low, he would have no choice but to cancel the shore assault.

Eugene Fluckey's last patrol as captain of *Barb* could end, as T. S. Eliot had written, "not with a bang but a whimper."

22 JULY 1945

> 1200 *Southerly breezes brought a stratus. At least the weather is right. Passed word that SABOTEURS will land tonight. After days of patiently waiting and observing, the undercurrent of expected action that ran through the boat made one's spine tingle.*
>
> 2145 *Trim dive.*
>
> 2155 *Surfaced, flooded down.*

2200 *Briefed SABOTEUR party. Headed in. The*
atmosphere is charged with excitement.
Rubber boats are being inflated, equipment
is being gathered, and last minute joshing is
well in progress. The night is perfect with a
moderate overcast hiding a 3/4 moon, so
that we have just enough light, the sea is calm and
the tide is slack.

They crept in toward shore on battery power, almost completely in silence. Any man on deck was to speak only in the quietest of whispers, if he needed to speak at all.

"Radar contact. Two small vessels coming down the coastline."

"All stop," Fluckey whispered. There were murmured curses from more than one man on the deck of the *Barb*.

The skipper maneuvered the boat as necessary to avoid the two interlopers. They did not have to move much since the submarine was flooded down to more easily launch the rubber boats. Without the moon, *Barb* looked much like a small schooner or patrol boat. Even so, Fluckey sent gun crews to battle stations, guns, but without the usual gongs clanging. It took forty-five minutes for what appeared to be a couple of sampans to meander on past.

23 JULY 1945

0000 *SABOTEUR ATTACK #1. In position at last. Two*
fathoms under the keel. Shore line 950 yards. We
can do no better. Launched rubber boats.

0005 *As boats shoved off had planned to say something*
apropos to such an operation as, "Synchronize
your watches," however all I could think of was,
"Boys, if you get stuck, head for Siberia 130 miles
north—follow the mountain ranges, good
luck."

It did not occur to Gene Fluckey that nobody in the history of submarine warfare had ever written in a patrol report the words "Saboteur attack," just as no one had ever ordered "battle stations—rockets" before he did, just three weeks earlier in the run.

The delay, waiting for the sampans to pass, meant that the men now had only about three hours to do their work and get back to the sub. *Barb* would have to leave and head for deeper water with the first glow of dawn. It would take the team a half hour each way to row to and from the boat. As much as they loved the eight men who were bravely going ashore, they could not risk the ship and the rest of the crew being in daylight this near enemy territory.

Tensions escalated, in the rubber boats and aboard *Barb*, as the saboteurs used their compasses to navigate toward the pre-determined landing point. There was soon a problem. They were to line up with a couple of twin mountain peaks in the distance, but by the time they were in the water and rowing, fog shrouded the landmark. The compasses were jumping around, too, likely due to all the metal they carried in the boats. They ultimately landed at the wrong spot, dangerously near a house. Luckily, there were no dogs there to alert the residents.

Then, with the two guards left behind, the other six hurried through the grassy meadow. The "grass" turned out to be noisy bullrushes that crackled and snapped much too loudly. They crossed the highway, but only after discovering four-foot-deep drainage ditches on either side. But they finally double-timed through the scrub to the tracks.

There was no sound but that of their own ragged breathing as they sat and rested a moment before getting busy. Three men moved off to act as guards, Markuson specifically dispatched to take a look at a tall tower down the tracks. The other three selected the best spot along the tracks and started digging. The manufactured picks and shovels made too much noise, though. They resorted to using their bare hands.

Then they heard the footsteps of someone running toward them in the darkness. All three men pointed pistols in that direction. But it was only Markuson, who appeared out of the blackness, eyes wide.

"Easy, boys," he muttered. "The only person you'll see running out here is a scared American."

He had returned to warn them that the tower was a Japanese Army guard post. Markuson had climbed up and peeked inside. There was a sentry in it, but he was sleeping soundly, snoring.

Just then, though, there was a more urgent threat. The rumble of an approaching train, barreling their way. The men scrambled, trying to find hiding places in the bushes. The train roared on past without slowing or giving any sign that anybody on board had seen the submariners, even though they could clearly see the engineer looking out in their direction.

With the urgency suddenly ratcheted up, they rushed to dig

the hole, then bury the scuttle charge and the pickle can that held the batteries. Then all the men—except for Billy Hatfield—scurried some distance away, lying on the ground curled up with their backs to any accidental conflagration that might occur. Meanwhile, Hatfield carefully placed the switch—purloined from the spare-parts supply of *Barb*'s radar crew—beneath the rail on a carefully constructed wooden wedge. Then, sure the device was only a half inch below the rail, he held his breath and carefully connected the wires from the switch to the battery and bomb.

No accidental blast. The device seemed ready.

When Hatfield looked up, once again breathing, all five of his shipmates were standing right behind him, watching him work. They wanted to be sure he did things right, they told him.

Back on the *Barb*, there had been near panic on the bridge when they saw the train approaching the spot where their saboteurs were likely working. Then nothing. Fluckey, Webster, and the lookouts also kept an eye on the beach, not sure exactly where the two boats had landed. No signs of the men guarding the boat. And no sighting of the Japanese soldier and his dog making one of their irregular patrols up the shoreline.

As Fluckey was growing even more concerned, someone spotted the red dots and dashes in the darkness along the beach, the signal that their guys were pushing away from the shore, headed back to the sub. Fluckey had already moved *Barb* even closer to land than he had intended. They had less than six feet of water beneath the keel. The captain wanted to get as close as he dared to give the team a slightly shorter return—no problem so long as *Barb* did not end up on a sandbar. The deck guns were manned, too.

"Another train coming, Captain!" One of the men at the fifty-caliber gun spoke just loud enough for Fluckey to hear his report from the bridge. Everyone on the submarine's deck could then see it. It was indeed a train, traveling fast in the same direction as the previous one. A long snake of a train.

The two rubber boats were about halfway between the beach and *Barb*. Fluckey grabbed his megaphone—the one he so often used to communicate from bridge to bridge with other members of his wolfpack—and made no attempt to remain quiet.

"Paddle like the devil, boys!" he shouted. The demolition team had seen the approaching train, too. They were, as Fluckey would later write, "paddling like eggbeaters."

At 1:47 in the morning, the rail cracked the walnut.

Everyone on the sub's bridge, as well as the men in the boats, were stunned by the intensity of the explosion. Fluckey later described what they had set loose.

"What a thrill! The flash of the charge exploding changed into a spreading ball of sparkling flame. The boilers of the engine blew. Engine wreckage flying, flying, flying up some two hundred feet, racing ahead of a mushroom of smoke, now white, now black. Cars piling up into and over the wall of wreckage in front, rolling off the track in a writhing, twisting maelstrom of Gordian knots."

It took several seconds for the sounds of the blast to reach the submarine. It was a resounding cacophony of thunder, screeching metal, and grinding mayhem.

Fluckey grabbed up his megaphone and shouted toward the rubber boats, "Hurry up! Paddle! We're leaving!"

When the last man was safely aboard, the captain ordered the submarine to turn around, to point the bow seaward. They made their escape at the not-so-blistering speed of two knots, careful not to deviate from the route they hoped would keep them off the bottom. Meanwhile, Fluckey got on the intercom system and invited everyone not on watch and busy to come topside. There, they could see fires still burning and the first military vehicles arriving at the scene, lights flashing.

As soon as *Barb* could safely dive, the crew assembled to splice the main brace. They also heard all the new sea stories the eight saboteurs were telling. Some of them were true.

Fluckey was not finished, of course. They still had extended patrol time available, some cutie torpedoes, and a bunch of rockets, too.

On July 24, they used up some of those rockets on the Patience Bay factory town of Shiritori. They set massive fires among the many facilities there, using a smokestack that Fluckey estimated to be four hundred feet tall as their point of aim. Later that night—early on the morning of July 25—they bombarded another bunch of factories and warehouses in Kashiho, again setting fires and blasting targets high into the predawn sky. They used up the last of the rockets.

As they moved away, Gene Fluckey told one of his officers that he had only one regret. He knew he had likely just given his last command of "Rockets away!"

The day prior to his final two rocket attacks, he received orders that came from the top—Admiral Lockwood—to end the patrol and head for Midway. Fluckey and his crew had done enough already. Fluckey pointed out to his XO that the message did not give a specific route home. The skipper elected to take a roundabout course to get back into the Pacific, one that just happened to take them past the factory towns of Shiritori and Kashiho. He remained within the letter of the command yet still had an opportunity to bash a couple of wonderful targets.

There would be more. Once they were finally pointed east, before leaving the coast of Sakhalin Island, determined to use up all their ammunition, they took down seven more sampans and knocked out a cannery at Chiri. They captured one survivor from one of the doomed sampans. The new POW shared an interesting news report he had heard: Allied aircraft had destroyed a train two nights before. He pointed out on a map the spot where it happened. Yes, it was the train *Barb*'s guys had blown up. A troop train, killing more than 150 soldiers. Once again, *Barb* had done her job but would get no formal credit for it.

As a final goodbye, on the way out of the Sea of Okhotsk, Fluckey wiped out a lumber mill and sampan factory, including an estimated thirty-five new boats—later confirmed to be fifty-nine—then afterward used a hand grenade launcher to set a trawler afire. When the trawler refused to sink, though, the skipper ordered it to be rammed by *Barb*. They did. Down the blazing vessel went, fortunately with no damage to the submarine beyond some scraped paint.

As they finally exited through Kunashiri Strait toward the Pacific, *Barb* once more passed that telegraph cable station that Fluckey had been craving since his first visit to these parts. As usual, it was hidden in thick fog. And, to be truthful, *Barb* lacked any ordnance to hurl that way had the installation been in the clear. No ammunition, shells, or rockets. Not even grenades for the launcher.

Unlike so many other targets north of the Home Island of Hokkaido, east of Sakhalin Island, in Patience Bay, and around the cold waters of the Sea of Okhotsk, that cable station would ultimately escape the ire of the Galloping Ghost.

But only because *Barb* ran out of bullets.

CHAPTER NINETEEN

"I LOVED THAT *BARB* GIRL"

2 AUGUST, 1945

1000   Arrived Midway; An excellent Welcome.

T hough the end of USS *Barb*'s twelfth war patrol also brought to a close Eugene Bennett Fluckey's days as a wartime submarine commanding officer, it did not mark the conclusion of his service to the Navy, his country, or his fellow man. The sub and crew arrived back at Midway Atoll on August 2, 1945, flying what had to be the most impressive battle flag in submarine history. The thing had kept several sailors busy on the trip home, stitching onto the pennant the patches to indicate the additional ships recently sunk by the *Barb*.

There were more than sixty patches on there for each ship sent to the bottom on her seven Pacific runs, dispatched by torpedoes as well as deck guns, plus ones for the rescued Allied prisoners of war and downed pilots. There were two emblems that had never graced a submarine battle flag; those represented the rocket attacks and the sabotage of the troop train on Karafuto.

But the smile on Gene Fluckey's face as they were warmly welcomed back to Midway was not only for their amazing action against the enemy. He pointed out that, despite the hundreds of depth charges, bombs, and shells dropped on his boat, throughout all the close calls in shallow water, and even after sending eight men into enemy territory to blow up a railroad, they had not suffered a single casualty. No Purple Hearts. And they were submariners, the branch of the service with the highest casualty rate of any in the war.

Fluckey and his crew had garnered a spectacular haul of hardware during his time as CO. The *Barb* was awarded the Presidential Unit Citation for her eighth, ninth, tenth, and eleventh runs, and the Navy Unit Commendation for the twelfth patrol. Members of the crew earned an unprecedented six Navy Crosses, twenty-three Silver Stars, and twenty-three Bronze Stars. And, of course, their skipper had received the Medal of Honor for the attack in Namkwan Harbor on the eleventh run.

Fluckey could also take satisfaction in knowing he had proven many of the points he wanted to make about the various uses of submarines in wartime: how to be aggressive without being foolhardy. Remaining on the surface for speed and a wider view. Using deck guns for assaults. Not ducking under at first sight of aircraft.

There were other submarine captains who helped Fluckey prove those points, and they had made a huge difference in how the war was going for the Japanese—skippers so aggressive and creative that their damage was often being attributed to aircraft or surface ships. No submarine had ever attempted what Fluckey and his contemporaries were doing.

He was even more a pioneer in other applications, though, such as noting the value of using submarines to deliver sabotage teams into enemy territory. Though it cannot be verified, common lore in the Navy is that there are usually eight men in a SEAL squad even today because *Barb* sent eight men ashore on those two rubber boats. It is certain, though, that the Navy saw the value in what Fluckey accomplished with his submarine and volunteer saboteurs. Most historians agree that the men off the *Barb* formed the only successful sabotage mission into the Japanese Home Islands in World War II. Nowadays, SEAL teams operate extensively with submarines employed as delivery platforms, placing them near the beach in dangerous territory to conduct their daring missions.

Fluckey's prediction that torpedoes would cease to be a primary weapon employed by submarines has not yet come to pass and may well not. However, the boats are now a primary means of carrying and launching powerful ballistic missiles—nuclear ballistic missiles. The value of that stealthy deterrence is inestimable.

The final war patrol report for *Barb*'s twelfth run would be more than a hundred pages long, typed and single-spaced, one of the most comprehensive—and fascinating—of any such report in the war. It included extremely detailed descriptions of each running, gunning attack. It would have made fascinating reading for the president of the United States, Franklin Roosevelt.

But it was not to be. Roosevelt had died in April in Warm Springs, Georgia.

Harry Truman, Roosevelt's vice president, had become

commander in chief upon FDR's death. When faced with the potential for millions of deaths should the planned Allied invasion of the Home Islands be carried out, Truman chose another option. He authorized the dropping of an atomic bomb on a target in Japan in an effort to convince the enemy to accept articles of surrender.

The bomb fell on the city of Hiroshima at about eight a.m. on the morning of August 6, 1945. When the news came, USS *Barb* was still in port at Midway as Commander Fluckey went through the process of turning over the boat to her new skipper, Lieutenant Commander Patrick Callahan. *Barb* was to be based next in Guam, where Admiral Nimitz and Admiral Lockwood had now established the Navy's Pacific war headquarters. The sub's next patrol was supposed to be lifeguard duty between the Marianas and Japan, supporting the massive incendiary bomb runs by US aircraft off Tinian, Saipan, and Guam. Horrible destruction and loss of life from those raids had so far not convinced the Japanese to surrender.

Barb's crew stayed close to their radio, waiting for updates on the awful new bomb. Though details were sparse, it was clear the single weapon that hit Hiroshima had done unprecedented destruction and the loss of human life was stunning. Even so, Gene Fluckey was not sure it would be enough for the Japanese to capitulate. And he feared it might push the Empire to attempt some kind of desperate, suicidal effort.

He suggested to Pat Callahan that they go ahead and conduct the change-of-command ceremony so *Barb* would be prepared to head out on short notice. Or, if the emperor finally saw the writing on the wall and waved the white flag, Callahan would at least have a wartime submarine command on his record, even if it was only for a few hours, days, or weeks. Though such a changeover in commanding officers was typically a ten-day process, Callahan gratefully agreed.

Fluckey had another request for his relief. He admitted that the ceremony, saying goodbye to his crew in front of all the top brass at Midway, might be too emotional for him. He suggested they do the event somewhere besides the deck of *Barb*, with the crew at muster looking on, as would have been typical. The only place available was the base bar.

With his officers and chief of the boat Paul "Swish" Saunders there, attired in their dress uniforms, Fluckey read his orders aloud, Callahan read his, the two men shook hands, and Callahan said, "I relieve you, sir." With that, they proceeded to splice the main brace with champagne, signed for by Eugene Fluckey, the former skipper of USS *Barb*. So far as we can tell, this was yet another first for the submarine service, a change-of-command ceremony conducted in a bar.

The next day, August 8, Russia finally declared war on Japan. Despite their tardiness in entering the fray, Russia would eventually be granted in the peace settlement territory including Sakhalin Island and the Kuriles, including the Sea of Okhotsk and Patience Bay. Eugene Fluckey would later term this a "robbery" by the Russians and added, "I was happy the *Barb* had destroyed a part of it."

One day later, on August 9, at about ten a.m., a second atomic bomb fell on a major Japanese urban area, Nagasaki, the port city near where *Barb* had done some of her prime hunting on her eleventh patrol. After intense internal discussions and an attempted coup against him by elements of the military, Japanese Emperor Hirohito addressed the nation by radio—the first time many Japanese had heard his voice—announcing his intent to surrender to the Allies. A formal signing of the surrender agreement would occur three weeks later, on September 2, aboard the battleship USS *Missouri* (BB-63) in Tokyo Bay.

Though hostilities would officially end at that event, Admiral Nimitz had already declared that offensive operations by any US Navy unit were to cease on August 15. Even so, Pat Callahan and *Barb* were ordered to proceed on to Guam, just in case Japan tried something, and to cautiously conduct training exercises along the way. There was speculation among the Allies that Hirohito might not have total control over his nation's military and that elements of the military would not willingly lay down their arms.

At ten a.m. on August 21, 1945, Commander Eugene Fluckey was on the pier as *Barb* took in all lines and slowly pulled away. Fluckey lifted the final rope off a bollard and tossed it across to a sailor on the submarine. With tears in his eyes, he shouted, "Good luck, Pat. And God bless all you Barbarians!" He continued to wave—and men on the deck and bridge waved back—until the boat was out of sight.

"I loved that *Barb* girl," Fluckey later wrote.

In his report on the twelfth patrol, the CO had paid heartfelt homage to the men of the *Barb*. "How difficult it is to close this chapter of the *Barb*. What wordy praise can one give such men as these. Men who, without the information available to the CO follow unhesitatingly when in the vicinity of [a] minefield so long as there is the possibility of targets. Men who . . . land on Jap land, to blow up a Jap train with a self-trained demolition team. Men who flinch not with the fathometer ticking off 2 fathoms beneath the keel. Men who shout that the destroyer is running away after we've thrown every punch we possess and are getting our ears flattened back. Men who will fight to the last bullet and then want to start throwing empty shell cases."

Fluckey would later unequivocally maintain that no single World War II submarine or crew should be declared "the best." Ranking lists of various submarines and skippers that were determined by number of ships sunk, tonnage, and other damage would vary greatly, depending on unreliable and fuzzy sources and changeable criteria. Fluckey said that *Barb* was never in competition with any other boat or captain or patrol. She was in competition only with herself. His goal was to make each patrol better and more effective than the last. And, of course, to do what he could to end the war and return to his family.

Barb never made it to Guam. The day after Fluckey's emotional farewell, the boat received orders to return to Midway, then to proceed on to Pearl Harbor. The short round trip would not count as a "war patrol." From Hawaii, it was back through the Panama Canal, up the East Coast, and to New London. There the sub went into the reserve fleet, mothballed in April 1946.

In 1951, the submarine was reactivated, underwent modifications, and briefly served her country once again. But then, as with many of the World War II subs, she was sold to a foreign navy. *Barb* was renamed *Enrico Tazzoli* (S-511) and became a unit of the Italian navy in early 1955. The new namesake was an Italian priest, patriot, and martyr. The boat was decommissioned in 1972 and sold for scrap for about $100,000. At a crew reunion in later years, Fluckey told attendees that if he and the crew had known she was for sale, they would have bought the boat, towed her across the Atlantic, and made her a museum ship somewhere. As of this writing, there are fifteen US World War II submarines open to the public as museum ships around the country.

That distinctive *Barb* battle flag is now at the Submarine Force Library and Museum, located adjacent to the sub school on the banks of the Thames River in Groton, Connecticut. Another submarine named *Barb* (SSN-596), a nuclear-powered vessel, was in service from 1963 until 1989. Marjorie Fluckey was invited to sponsor and christen that ship at its launch in Pascagoula, Mississippi. In October of 2020, the US Navy announced that a new *Virginia*-class submarine (SS-804) would be built and would be named for USS *Barb*.

From his teary goodbye to his crew at Midway, Gene Fluckey went straight to a waiting airplane and a ride to Hawaii. With the war all but officially at an end, the Navy had released to the media some of the highlights of *Barb*'s last two spectacular runs. Reporters met Fluckey as soon as he climbed off a bumpy flight across the Pacific. He and his exploits were featured in an article in *Time* magazine and on a live broadcast on the NBC radio network. Gene was worried that now that word was out, Marjorie would be mad at him for playing down in his letters to her the battle action in which he had been involved.

In Hawaii, with the war over and Lockwood's staff being reduced, Fluckey received orders to once again command a submarine. He was to put into commission one of the first post–World War II boats, the USS *Dogfish* (SS-350), and be based in Groton, all of which suited him perfectly. But it was not to be. His orders changed again. He was to join the staff of the man who had handed him the Medal of Honor, Secretary of the Navy James Forrestal, and he would be based in his hometown, Washington, DC. At the last minute, that fell through as well.

Then came a call from Admiral Chester Nimitz, who had just been named chief of naval operations. He knew Fluckey from the visit at the curb in front of the Royal Hawaiian Hotel in Honolulu with the president, General MacArthur, and Admiral Lockwood. Their paths had crossed another time or two, and he was obviously aware of Fluckey's record on *Barb*. Now he wanted Fluckey to become his aide. The submarine hero accepted, thus beginning what Fluckey thought of as a father-son relationship. Nimitz and his wife soon became good friends with Gene and Marjorie during the year and a half they worked together.

But with politics driving change among the various branches of the armed forces, Admiral Nimitz moved to other duties. Gene Fluckey found himself back at the helm of a submarine, the USS *Halfbeak* (SS-352), homeported in New London. He and the girls made yet another move back to Connecticut in late 1947. He did not run the *Halfbeak* long before being promoted twice, in rapid succession, first to work with the naval reserve program, then to become flag secretary to the commander of the Atlantic submarine fleet. It was 1949 and the Soviet Union had also become a nuclear power, testing their first atomic bomb in August of that year. The Cold War was just getting cranked up. And Gene Fluckey, who had always mistrusted Russia, found himself on the front lines.

As part of the undeclared war, military relationships in Europe took on new importance. Russia was now in control of a big portion of Germany, with Berlin in the middle of that territory. In 1950, Fluckey was named military attaché at the American embassy in Portugal. That was to help keep an eye on things on that continent, but it also gave Gene, Marjorie, and Barbara their most stable three years together as a family.

Then, over the next several years, the Fluckeys were on the move again as he became commander of Submarine Division 52 in San Diego, skipper of the sub tender *Sperry*, and then commander of Submarine Squadron Five, overseeing all eighteen boats based around the Pacific. In that role, he was able to work with early testing of missile launches from submarines, using far more sophisticated equipment than the simple launchers and "bottle rockets" shot off the deck of *Barb* in the Sea of Okhotsk.

In 1956, after promotion to the rank of captain, he became head of the electrical engineering department at the US Naval Academy. By this time, Barbara was in school at the University of California in Berkley, and the family was separated yet again. Later he attended the National War College, became a rear admiral in 1960, then went through several command positions, including a stint as director of naval intelligence.

In 1968, Gene and Marjorie found themselves back in Portugal when he became the first commander of NATO's Iberian military operations. After their earlier time there, it was almost like going home, except Barbara was no longer with them. She had married and presented them with a grandchild.

Even so, when he reached the end of his time at the NATO facility in 1972, he decided to retire from the Navy and he and Marjorie remained in Portugal. There they dedicated themselves to helping take care of orphaned children.

Marjorie Fluckey died of cancer in August of 1979. They had been married for forty-two years. She and Gene had been staying with their daughter at her home in Crofton, Maryland, near Annapolis. Gene took his wife's ashes back to Portugal, where he scattered them about the garden at their home in the town of Sintra and on the grounds of the orphanage where they had spent so much time.

The next year, Fluckey remarried, wedding a British national named Margaret Wallace, introduced by mutual friends in Portugal. They soon moved back to Annapolis so Gene could be near his daughter and granddaughter, as well as the Naval Academy, but they continued to travel extensively, including while Gene did research for his book. In 1989, a six-story research facility at the submarine school in New London was named Fluckey Hall in his honor. Another building, this one at the submarine base at Kings Bay, Georgia, was named Fluckey Hall in 1995. Then another Fluckey Hall was opened in 1996 at the headquarters of US Submarine Group Seven at Yokosuka Naval Base in Japan. He and Margaret attended all three dedications.

Fluckey released his book, *Thunder Below!*, detailing his days as skipper of USS *Barb*, in 1992. Royalties from the sale of the book were set aside to help defray the expenses of former crew-members who wanted to attend reunions.

During this time, Fluckey was visited by a military artifacts collector who wanted to have a look at the admiral's many medals. The collector seemed impressed and volunteered to construct Fluckey a display case to properly exhibit the medals to visitors to his home. But the man said he needed to take them with him so he could properly custom design the case. Fluckey agreed.

Later, the man returned and had, indeed, built a nice case, with the Medal of Honor properly highlighted. Several months later, Fluckey received a call from the FBI. They asked him if he was aware that his Medal of Honor was being offered for sale on the black market for $30,000. Fluckey checked the medal in his new display case and could immediately tell it was not his, that it was fake. It did not have "Marjorie" engraved on the back. The thieving collector was arrested and served time. And Gene Fluckey had yet another good story to tell.

In 1999, Eugene Fluckey was diagnosed with Alzheimer's disease. After a long fight, one he was destined to lose, he died on June 28, 2007. He is buried at the Naval Academy in Annapolis.

As of this writing, only one World War II recipient of a Medal of Honor is still living. He is former Marine Woody Williams, now 98 years old, a hero of the Battle of Iwo Jima.

Perhaps Fluckey's best epitaph is a quote from an interview with him that appeared in the *Submarine Review*, a publication of the Naval Submarine League. His words were intended as advice for upcoming submariners but could certainly be of value to anyone.

He said, "Serve your country well. Put more into life than you expect to get out of it. Drive yourself and lead others. Make others feel good about themselves. They will outperform your expectations, and you will never lack for friends."

As I have mentioned in the author's notes for each of my other nonfiction historical works, any author takes a chance when they create quotes from or thoughts by individuals who are no longer around to verify their accuracy. In my case, I employ these devices to help the reader have more insight into the personalities, places, and times about which I write. It adds to the understanding and color of the story. I base those quotes and thoughts on well-researched reality. I locate as many oral histories as I can or interview those who were actually there and a part of the action. The latter is, of course, becoming more and more difficult with survivors of World War II.

Thanks to two invaluable sources, verifying thoughts and words was not nearly so much an issue in telling Admiral Fluckey's story. Fluckey did a book of his own, *Thunder Below!* (Urbana,

IL: University of Illinois Press, 1992), a personal account of the time in which he was skipper of USS *Barb*. He had also conducted extensive research for his book, including visiting Japan, looking at accounts of the actions in which he and his boat were involved from a different perspective, and meeting with men who were his adversaries in World War II. His work gives us a truly remarkable and personal record of what happened during that time, what he said and thought, as well as his research into and recollections of the words and actions of others.

As I have discovered with even the best oral histories, diaries, and other similar sources, they are not always totally accurate. Memories fade. Research is sometimes suspect. Events are embellished. Though I believe Admiral Fluckey's book to be remarkably accurate, including his recollections of his actions, thoughts, and conversations, I am thankful for a second primary source that has been helpful to me and obviously to Fluckey, too, since he heavily relied on the source for his book. This is the collection of the actual reports for submarine war patrols, compiled for every run by every sub in World War II. That includes *Barb*'s, especially the last five patrols that were so detailed and colorfully written at the time by Fluckey himself.

The reports were originally obtained on microfilm from the US Navy archives by the Naval Undersea Museum in Keyport, Washington, and made available there to researchers for in-person viewing and printing. That was a slow and cumbersome process. Former submariners John Clear and Dan Martini, with the permission of the museum, were eventually able to make all the reports available in PDF format on four compact discs. The scans are now also available for viewing at other submarine and naval museums around the country. Anyone can now easily access them. The complete set is available on the internet on the website of the Historic Naval Ships Association at hnsa.org /manuals-documents/submarine-war-reports. Many of them are remarkably entertaining as well as informative, especially those of the *Barb* from the eighth patrol through the twelfth.

Another source that helped confirm information for me was the book *The Galloping Ghost: The Extraordinary Life of Submarine Legend Eugene Fluckey* (Annapolis, MD: Naval Institute Press, 2007) by Carl LaVO.

Any author writing about World War II submarining simply has to rely heavily on Clay Blair Jr.'s exhaustive history, *Silent Victory: The U.S. Submarine War against Japan* (Annapolis, MD: Naval Institute Press, 2001). To assist me in picturing and describing the submarines in the story, I relied on the book *The World's Greatest Submarines: An Illustrated History* (London: Amber Books Ltd., 2017) by David Ross.

Finally, I also used research material and the many interviews I have conducted while writing my previous books on World War II submarines. That includes *Final Patrol: True Stories of World War II Submarines* (New York: NAL Caliber, 2006), which tells the stories of each of the World War II boats that are open to the public as museum ships, and *Undersea Warrior: The World War II Story of "Mush" Morton and the USS* Wahoo (New York: NAL Caliber, 2011).

I always strive for accuracy and I also try to breathe a bit of true life into these fascinating individuals who are no longer here to tell their stories. I often point out that I do not write about submarines or ships, airplanes or tanks. I write about seemingly ordinary people who are placed in unusual situations and then do remarkable things.

It took (and still takes) a unique person to volunteer to serve aboard submarines. Eugene Bennett Fluckey certainly qualified. I hope I have been able to bring him and the crew of *Barb* to life for you.

Don Keith
Indian Springs Village, Alabama